Linda Lovelace
OUT OF BONDAGE

Linda Lovelace

OUT OF
BONDAGE

with Mike McGrady

c. 1

LYLE STUART INC.
Secaucus, New Jersey

B

LOVELACE, L,

Library of Congress Cataloging-in-Publication Data

Lovelace, Linda.
  Out of bondage.

    1. Lovelace, Linda.   2. Women social reformers—
United States—Biography.   3. Housewives—United States—
Biography.   4. Pornography—Social aspects—United
States—Case studies.   1. McGrady, Mike.   II. Title.
HQ1413.L68A36   1986   305.4'2'0924   86-1921
ISBN 0-8184-0386-1

Published by Lyle Stuart Inc.
120 Enterprise Ave., Secaucus, N.J. 07094
In Canada; Musson Book Company
A division of General Publishing Co. Limited.
Don Mills, Ontario

Queries regarding rights and permissions should be
addressed to: Lyle Stuart, 120 Enterprise Avenue.
Secaucus, N.J. 07094

Manufactured in the United States of America

*This is dedicated to
the ones I love*

introduction

I am writing an introduction to this book by and about my friend, Linda Marchiano, for reasons that have everything to do with you, the reader.

First, I want to strike a bargain. If you begin her story, please read it to the end. If you know only part of Linda's experience, I fear that you will be left wondering if she could have brought some part of her tragedy upon herself.

I don't say this because I lack faith in the reader. On the contrary, I believe you can and will judge the humiliating facts of her long journey for yourself. That's precisely why *Out of Bondage*—like her earlier book, *Ordeal*—is so very important.

But we are too close to the time when even rape victims were suspected of "asking for" the crimes of humiliation and violence inflicted upon them; a time when the testimony of a victim was disbelieved unless corroborated by witnesses who had watched the crime, and a victim's past personal life was admissable in court when the rapist's past, even if criminal, was not.

No wonder we are still in a time when the thousands of teenage runaways, terrified women and even children who are victims of forced prostitution and pornography each year—

victims who are forced to coexist and depend for their lives on their victimizers for far longer than the duration of a rapist's attack—are accused of cooperating with their captors, even of enjoying their own humiliation, or at least of being suspect because they did not escape.

After all, millions of viewers saw *Deep Throat*, the first hardcore porn film to enter the popular culture, without asking whether the young woman known as "Linda Lovelace" was there of her own free will. They ignored the bruises that were visible on her body, the terror in her eyes, even the simple empathy that should cause each of us to wonder whether another human being really could enjoy humiliations and dangers that we ourselves would never tolerate. Linda was forced to smile, but viewers were not forced to accept that smile.

How much harder will it be to believe the long road back to self-respect, when Linda was physically free but still imprisoned by society's opinion of her, that is the subject of this book?

Second, I want to offer my own support as a journalist, and later as a friend, for the facts of Linda's story: her captivity against her will, her attempts to escape, and her many efforts to be believed so that her story would help not only herself but others forced into pornography and prostitution.

She should not need this support. As you soon will read, she had been put through many factual proofs, including a long and grueling set of lie detector tests, long before we met. They were the precondition of publisher Lyle Stuart and of journalist Mike McGrady, her co-author, before the publication of *Ordeal*. Furthermore, those who have protested her story, even threatened her because of it, have yet to deliver proof that counters any part of it.

But her story was so widely ridiculed, so disbelieved by critics who accused her of seeking publicity or even of masochistically enjoying the sexual tortures that have scarred her body, that I, too, re-investigated the facts before writing a 1980 article* for *Ms.* Magazine when *Ordeal* was first published. I also interviewed Linda myself, watched her undergo many other media interviews by reporters proud of their ability to detect pretense and inconsistencies, listened to her trying to help other women escaping from pasts of prostitution and pornography, and, finally, came to know the private Linda as she dealt with husband and friends, or cared for one child and gave birth to another.

Six years of knowing her have strengthened my early conclusion as a reporter: that she is telling the truth. In the interim, I have added only one modification: that she may be telling it with restraint and generosity. For instance: Linda left out of *Ordeal* a number of incidents involving Hugh Hefner and his Playboy Mansion in Los Angeles, even though they were newsworthy incidents of sex and celebrity. Why? Because she was not positive that Hefner knew she was a prisoner, acting under threat of death by her "husband" and keeper, at the time.

How does this sense of fairness survive inside someone who has been treated so unfairly? That is the miracle. I no longer question whether the reasons for her ordeal might lie within herself, her acts, her background: there is no doubt in my mind that the same thing could have happened to me, to anyone, had we had the similar bad luck of crossing the wrong person's path at the right time. (To say otherwise is no different from blaming a rape victim for her walk, her dress.) What *is* exceptional about Linda is her ability to escape, to survive, to live.

Third, I want to remind all of us that to condemn pornography is not to condemn sex, nor even to condone censorship. The question is freewill: Are the subjects of pornography there by choice, or by coercion, economic or physical? Are viewers seeking out pornography by choice, or are they forced to confront it in the public streets, newsstands and airways?

---

* Reprinted as "The Real Linda Lovelace" in *Outrageous Acts and Everyday Rebellions*, Holt, Rinehard and Winston hardcover, New American Library paperback.

In fact, we have a First Amendment right to demonstrate against pornography, to boycott its creators and sellers, to explain that pornography is to women of all groups what Nazi literature is to Jews and Ku Klux Klan literature is to Blacks. It is as different from erotica as sex is different from rape. After all, *porné* means harlot, prostitute or female captive; thus, pornography is the writing about or depiction of female sexual slavery. On the other hand, *eros* means sexual love, and love implies free choice and mutual pleasure. The point is to separate sex from violence, pleasure from pain.

Finally, I would like to make one more bargain with you. When you've finished this book, walk through the center for prostitution and pornography that probably exists in your city or town—and figure out how you can protest it.

Ask yourself if friends, even family members may be supporting pornography by buying or tolerating it—and let them know this is just as offensive as supporting anti-Semites or the Klan. Get up the courage to say how you feel, to throw pornography out of your life and house at least. Educate your children in the difference between pornography and erotica, between domination and mutual choice. Support the centers that are helping women and children escape this coercion and find self-respect.

The miracle is that Linda has survived to tell her story.

The rest is up to us.

GLORIA STEINEM

one

─────────────

I'm back in my bedroom in a rented cottage in Beverly Glen, California. The window beside my bed is open. A small noise there causes me to stir. I look up through sleepy eyes and see a man, a stranger, and he's crawling in through my window. I try to scream but my throat is paralyzed. I want to run but my legs have lost all strength. As I sit up in bed, I see the other men, five of them, all strangers, all surrounding my bed, staring down at me. I know what is to follow—the beating and the raping—and a terrible panic overwhelms me, leaving me weak and helpless. I start to sob wildly, uncontrollably.

It is then that I wake up.

I rarely have the dream any more. But just a few years ago the dream came every night. I dreaded sleep because those men would always be there, surrounding my bed, waiting, threatening.

The dream comes from an earlier life—back when I was Linda Lovelace, the star of *Deep Throat*, the high princess of pornography. Most likely the dream springs from a specific incident, a hot summery day when a man named Chuck Traynor introduced me to prostitution by selling me

11

to five men in a motel room in Florida. And every time I have the dream, I'm forced to go through feelings of fear and pain, of helplessness and hopelessness.

There was no escaping those feelings. Even when the dream ended, the memories would be there. I would wake up battered by a nightmare and the flashback would begin.

Flashback to—

A Holiday Inn in South Miami, a sprawling two-story building not far from the University of Miami. Walking with Chuck down the central corridor, up a flight of stairs, down another hallway to the end. The last room, Chuck knocking on the door three times, a man staring out at us, smiling, letting us in. Five men in the room, middle-aged, businessmen, wearing ties and jackets, having a drink, giving me the old once-over. Chuck talking to me in the dressing room, saying, "Those five guys out there—you're going to fuck every one of them" Me looking for the joke: "Chuck don't talk crazy." No joke: "You got no fucking choice. I already got the money. And that's something I want you to remember. The first thing you do is get the money . . . now take off your clothes."

Saying no, then seeing the gun in Chuck's hand, listening to his insanity; "You know what I think? I think you're going to take off your clothes, all of your clothes, and then you're going to go out there and fuck those five guys. And if you don't I'm gonna put a bullet in your head right now."

And me, still innocent, still looking for a smile but seeing only a gun. "I'm gonna shoot you right now unless you get out there and do what I'm telling you." Knowing that he meant it, he wasn't lying; he would shoot me. Going numb then, the tears flooding my eyes as I remove my clothes, trembling, really shaking, too frightened to even pray. Chuck saying: "Stop your crying before you go out there. Crying is bad for business." Walking out into the room then, wearing nothing. A man coming over and putting his hands on my breasts: "Not bad. Chuck got us a nice young one this time."

The story of that day, that life, was told in an earlier book, *Ordeal*. In those days your worst nightmares were my everyday occurrences. For nearly three years I was enslaved by Traynor, a man who beat me and kicked me; a man who hypnotized me and sold me and traded me; a man who managed finally to turn me into a sexual zombie, able to do anything while feeling nothing.

The nightmares didn't end in 1973 with my escape from Chuck Traynor. *Deep Throat* was behind me; enslavement was behind me; a great deal was behind me. No longer was I forced to have sex with strangers for pay. No longer was I a party favor given freely to celebrities. However, although I was away from that life, I was not free of it. My nights were filled with dreams and my days were crowded with ghosts.

I was Chuck's profitable little sexual zombie and he wasn't about to give me up without a fight. He searched for me everywhere, and I had to go into hiding. Wherever Chuck went in those days, he carried a flight bag concealing a semi-automatic revolver. While I was hiding out, protected by professional bodyguards, I was shown a newspaper story about Chuck.

"She's either going to work for me or she'll work for nobody," I read. "I'll see to that. She's mistaken if she thinks she's going to do her nightclub act without me. . . . I've made her what she is today. She'd be nothing without me."

It took a long time for my fear of Chuck to dissolve. Over and over again I tried to tell people what I had gone through—that I'd been brutalized, that I'd been a victim, that none of it was my idea—but no one wanted to hear that. Newspaper reporters couldn't write the truth because it would be "too libelous"; a well-known television host rapidly changed the subject; a publisher explained that the truth was too downbeat and would never sell as well as the fiction they had published about me in the past; even family and friends seemed cool and disinterested. The whole story was taken lightly and before long I stopped boring people with it.

In those days the truth could only be found in fragments. *Playboy*, for example, allowed that Chuck Traynor "played a sort of porn Svengali to the early Linda's Trilby."

One person who knew the truth was Gerry Damiano, director of *Deep Throat*. Although Damiano avoids interviews, he was talking about Chuck Traynor to a college audience and his remarks found their way into the Boston *Phoenix*: "That man (Chuck Traynor) was a nothing. He had no personality, no charm, no brains. He was just a user of people and he used Linda. He gave her nothing and abused her. He was very brutal with her. . . . Many times she'd come on the set and be completely black and blue."

Isn't that amazing! Reading that gave me a classic set of mixed emotions. On the one hand: Thank God *someone* finally backed up my story. On the other hand: why didn't he do something at the time; why didn't he come to my rescue?

People always ask me why I didn't get help. *Where would I have gotten help? From whom would I have gotten help?* Here's Damiano admitting that he knew I was beaten viciously—yet he never lifted a finger to help me. He was by no means the only one.

Chuck never broke stride. Within a few weeks he was back at the old stand, managing—and later marrying—the second most famous pornographic star in the world, Marilyn Chambers, the former "Ivory Snow Girl." Marilyn Chambers began her porno career starring in *Behind the Green Door* and went on from there to ever bigger, ever more rotten movies.

It was impossible to get Traynor out of my mind. Because no matter what he did to me, no matter what crimes he committed in the past, he was free to wander wherever he wanted. And where he did a lot of his wandering was in front of the cameras.

Never alone. Alone, Chuck Traynor is less than nothing. So always he was seen with his current charge in tow. At first I felt Chuck and Marilyn were made for each other, that this was a match made in some strange porno heaven. But as I read the news accounts about the two of them, it seemed clear that Chuck was re-creating the same master-slave relationship he had with me. And the fact that "she smiles a lot" or "she looks like she likes it" has absolutely nothing to do with anything.

I watched the two of them on television and listened to Marilyn Chambers saying exactly the same things I used to say—how she lives for sex, how she can never get enough of that wonderful stuff, etc.—and I knew who was the author of both the lines and the sentiments.

The more I read about them, the more I could see Chuck was up to his old tricks. And the reporters who interviewed them seemed to notice that something was not quite right; to some it was like interviewing Edgar Bergen and Charlie McCarthy.

Ken Mayer in the Boston *Herald-American*: "Someone should tell Marilyn Chambers' manager Chuck Traynor that when a writer interviews his property, he should sit back, collect his 10 percent and zip his lip. . . . Traynor should take a crash course on getting lost."

A story in the Los Angeles *Free Press* noted that Chuck did the talking while Marilyn did the giggling: "Whenever asked to comment on something related to her sexual experiences or the making of her hard-core features, Marilyn would giggle and defer to Chuck's more businesslike demeanor."

The San Antonio *Express* quoted Marilyn's tribute to Chuck's "transformational skill": " 'Chuck changed my whole appearance,' Miss chambers swallows her beer. 'He taught me to be a lady.' And what is a lady? 'A lady,' says Miss Chambers gravely, 'A lady is someone who looks good. And doesn't speak unless she's spoken to.' "

The most ominous note appeared in a column written by
Larry Fields of the Philadelphia *News*. Traynor, as usual,
was doing all the talking. "Hovering by Marilyn's side was
her lover-manager-Svengali Chuck Traynor. . . . Marilyn
interrupted to ask for permission to go to the bathroom.
'Not right now,' Traynor said." When Marilyn asked a
second time, Traynor snapped at her, "Just sit there and
shut up." When Larry Fields urged Traynor to let her go to
the bathroom, Traynor turned on the columnist and
snarled, "I don't tell you how to write your columns. Don't
tell me how to treat my broads."

Now *that's* vintage Chuck. In Larry Fields's world, the
world most of us take for granted, these kinds of things do
not happen. Adults do not ask each other for permission to
go to the bathroom. But for two years, if I wanted to go to
the bathroom or read a magazine or file my nails, I asked
permission first.

I didn't have enough feeling left to feel sorry for Marilyn
Chambers. Besides—thank God!—the pressure was off me.
It took a court order to accomplish it, but Chuck was leaving me alone. Finally, I could come out of hiding and
be . . . what? I had no idea. Be myself, I guess. But who
was that?

Everyone seemed to think I would just go back and be
Linda Lovelace again, that I would star in pornographic
movies and distribute my sexual favors as freely as Chuck
had done. Only this time around, naturally, I'd be able to
keep the profits for myself.

Everyone wanted me to do the same thing. Famous
lawyers and high-priced accountants offered to set my
affairs straight—and then they'd say why don't we get a bottle of champagne and maybe we can talk it over in front of
the fireplace. This always came as a shock; still, it almost
always came.

One acquaintance who was selling cocaine said, "Hey, all
we have to do is get together and you don't have to pay a
thing."

The person I knew best and trusted most had just one message for me: *Go for it!* She would say, "You've already done it—what difference could it possibly make now? You can clean up, you can have a ball."

two

I was getting plenty of offers but they weren't the kind of offers I wanted. Offers like: "There's this guy over at MGM—if you're nice to him, he'll be nice to you." Offers like: "I know a vice president at Universal who will use you in a comedy and all he wants is a little deep throat." Offers like: "All you have to do is throw in one little deep-throat scene and the producer will kick in an extra $40,000."

No one could understand my reluctance. At this point it must have seemed as though I had nothing to lose. They explained that this was the way things had always been done in Hollywood, and after all, it's not as though I was still a virgin.

I listened to everyone and thought it over. And the first thing I did was establish lines that I wouldn't cross, no matter what. For example, there would be no more sex for someone else's entertainment or benefit. No matter what the world thought of me, I had never willingly been a whore and I was not going to start now.

That was never a real temptation. I can remember at least a dozen times when *Playboy* mogul Hugh Hefner tried to set me up with himself and one of his super-bunnies. But that kind of thing was never going to be my kind of thing again.

What lines *didn't* I draw? Well, I had completed an idiotic little R-rated movie entitled *Linda Lovelace for President* and that didn't bother me too much. I posed for a nude spread in *Playboy* and that didn't disturb me. Nudity was not really a big issue, not after all I'd been through. Very little mattered to me at this time. Whether I made money or not, whether I showed up for court dates or not, whether I was seen nude or not—none of that really mattered.

After Chuck's departure, my new advisers wanted me to walk around in transparent clothing. I did what I was told. When they wanted me to go to the opening of Ascot in England in a see-through dress, it never occurred to me not to do it.

It was all carefully explained to me. Public nudity was part of my "transition process," the gradual transition from pornography to movie stardom. After all, I couldn't just start dressing like a nun, could I? Once you've lost your self-esteem, it takes quite a while to get it back. For a long time I remained a robot, doing just what my new advisers told me to do.

And so what if I wore a see-through dress That was better than being thrown into a room with a dozen men and having a dildo inserted into every opening. No, the nudity really didn't bother me at all.

And what of the future? I hadn't the slightest idea. I'd never had a chance to become acquainted with myself. I'd gone directly from my parents' home to Chuck Traynor's world of prostitution and pornography and I had no idea what made me tick.

In effect, I had never been more than a visitor in the real world, the normal workaday world. During the past few years I had done little more than practice and perfect every perversion known to this civilization. Still immature, still unable to stand on my own two feet, I had been cast out into a world I didn't know at all.

In the year 1973, I was undoubtedly the most widely

known sex star in the world. In fact, by this time I had graduated from sex symbol to sexual caricature, from national scandal to national joke. (*Playboy* even printed a full page of Linda Lovelace jokes. Example: "We suppose it's only a matter of time before some pharmaceutical house comes out with Linda Lovelace Lovers' Quarrel Pills—to be taken when someone you ate disagrees with you.")

I felt like an ex-convict who has spent his entire life behind bars and one day is turned out, blinking, into the sunlight. Just that suddenly I found myself away from my captor and among people who had never experienced the terror I took for granted. I was standing there, not knowing which way to turn. I knew who I was *not* but I had no idea who I *was*—other than being confused and scared and alone.

Perhaps not quite alone. In those days I had one constant companion. Her name was Linda Lovelace—and there seemed no way for me to get rid of her. I smiled her slightly crooked smile and spoke in her soft voice and it was only natural that people would mix up the two of us. As a result of this confusion—because people thought that I was she and that she was I—I always needed protection.

I needed someone to keep the crowds away. I needed lawyers to protect me (often from other lawyers); I needed accountants to collect (and give out) my money; and I desperately needed a normal man in my life, someone to discourage the creeps, and to hold me when the nightmares came.

But Linda Lovelace was a valuable property and men could not seem to behave in a normal way around her. They wouldn't leave her alone, not when so much easy money was within easy reach. True enough, I no longer had to perform perverted sex acts with everyone Chuck Traynor nominated. But it's also true that I was still a long way from starring in either a remake of *Gone With the*

Wind or the new *Gidget Goes Ga Ga*. As my new advisers kept telling me, it was going to be a slow process, this climb to respectability.

How right they were! But neither they nor I realized the climb would take a full decade. Until those first decent propositions came along, I had to take some of what was offered. This meant going to England and wearing see-through clothes. That meant going to Harvard and accepting a special award from the boys ("To that actor or actress most willing to flout convention and risk worldly damnation in the pursuit of artistic fulfillment"). That meant tackling a stage play in Philadelphia and subjecting myself to the kind of reviews, as one writer saw it, that "An Egyptian President might expect if he were playing Tel Aviv."

And it meant going on and giving the same kind of interviews I had always given: "I think sex is beautiful. I think love is beautiful! I don't believe in censorship at all in any way, shape or form." However, those words were no longer ringing true. As one perceptive reporter noted, "The more you question Linda Lovelace, the more you wonder whether she really believes all the things she is saying or whether someone told her to say them. . . . It seems obvious that somebody has just put some ideas into her head."

At that time—just after completing *Linda Lovelace for President*—I was living in a rented home in California. It was quite expensive even though a tub in the upstairs bathroom had started to poke one leg through the livingroom ceiling. My car was a leased Bentley, burgundy in color, slightly more expensive than the house. I was spending money faster than it was coming in.

* * *

This was the woman Larry Marchiano got to know in late 1973. Actually, it was our second meeting. I had met Larry several years earlier in my pre-Chuck Traynor years. I looked upon him as part of the world I had grown up in, the world that had housed me during the first twenty-one years of my life. It was a world of quiet suburban homes and Saturday football games and high school dances. It was a world where people went steady, got engaged and married and raised children and worked hard for a living.

I have to wonder what Larry Marchiano thought when he saw me again, this time as a Hollywood "star." I know this much: His first opinion could not have been too high.

Late that year I went to Florida for legal reasons. I've been involved in so many court cases, I no longer remember exactly which one this was. Not that it matters much today. All that mattered about that trip was that I became reacquainted with the man who still shares my life.

three

During that Florida trip, I stayed with my parents. My X-rated career had been a source of pain and embarrassment to them. My father had once gone to see *Deep Throat*. I later heard from others that his reaction had been the logical one—he walked out of the theater and vomited. My mother may have suffered some mixed feelings; she asked me to send her photographs of myself autographed to the people at the country club where she worked.

This was something we could never talk about directly. I think maybe now, at this late date, my father might like to learn about that chapter of my life—just the other night on the phone he started asking me questions that go back to those days. He's never been able to read *Ordeal*, but he will someday. It's going to hurt him. He's going to cry, I know that.

One time he did say to me, "Why didn't you ever tell me

what was going on when you and Chuck would visit us?" I
had to explain that Chuck Traynor had threatened me: If I
told, he'd kill my whole family and then he'd kill me.

When I saw Larry Marchiano again, I felt an immediate . . . something for him. One reason: He was so unlike
most of the men I'd seen the past few years in Hollywood.
He had no airs. He wore casual clothes, not a monogram
in sight. At this point in his life (he'd just been laid off as
an installer of television cable) he was working part-time as
an apprentice plumber in Florida. He was also in the process of winding up a long relationship with another woman.

Sometimes you meet someone and it's a nice simple: Hi-
how-are-you? With someone else it can be: Oh-oh-better-
watch-out. There was something definitely going on with
Larry, an attraction. And my first reaction was cautious. I
purposely avoided looking at him or allowing his eyes to
meet my own.

What Larry saw was someone who had apparently "gone
Hollywood"; I was dropping celebrity names right and left,
talking a big game. But it was all bogus. He had only to
ask a few questions to learn that I had little real understanding of what was going on. And the minute I started
talking about my business affairs, he could see we were in
the same financial boat.

Larry Marchiano's own position in life could not have
been more humble. However, though I was a movie star,
an alleged author of best-selling paperbacks and an inter-
nationally known celebrity, I had no more money saved
than he did. Actually, the same amount. Zero.

I needed someone trustworthy to manage my affairs. At
first I had no idea that someone might be Larry, but I did
sense he could be trusted. And less than a week later, I
trusted him enough to ask whether he would come out to
California and take charge of my business affairs. That
must've sounded slightly more attractive than the job he
held—that day he had been carrying toilets into condomini-
ums under construction. He agreed to join me.

Why did I need someone else? Why couldn't I handle my own affairs? For nearly three years I had someone doing crazy things to me. You don't, after that time, suddenly start making your own decisions. I had fallen into a pattern of letting someone else decide everything about my life.

I had to get in touch with me. And at the time I didn't feel too badly off. My life was a real improvement over what it had been. Okay, I could never turn back the clock to my days at Maria Regina High School, but I could try and get in touch with what I really felt about things.

And what I really felt from the beginning was a certainty about Larry Marchiano's character and strength. He, however, could only be confused about me. And that made two of us.

During my brief stay in Florida, I managed to add to that confusion. Sammy Davis, Jr., happened to be there, starring in a nightclub revue. Readers of *Ordeal* will remember that Sammy Davis, Jr., had been very much a part of my life when I was Chuck Traynor's slave.

In Chuck's eyes, it had been a simple mathematical equation: Sammy Davis, Jr., was a big Hollywood celebrity; therefore, Sammy Davis, Jr., was to be cultivated; therefore, I was to do whatever he wanted whenever he wanted it.

Why would I take Larry and my family to see Sammy Davis, Jr., perform? Why would I then invite them to Sammy's hotel suite for a post-performance party? I think it shows just how confused I was—how much I wanted someone to care about me—thinking they'd be impressed by my famous show-business friends. But—and I shouldn't be surprised by this—just the opposite happened.

In the first place, Larry Marchiano has never been the kind of person who is impressed by superficial things. He had come to see Sammy Davis, Jr., perform—but he was not particularly happy with the crowd that gathered later for drinks in the entertainer's suite.

Larry and I were seated together at a table and he went to get some food from the buffet. No sooner was he gone than a stranger sat down beside me and started making conversation. Larry returned with my plate and saw the stranger talking to me.

"Hey, you," he said, "you're sitting in my seat."

"Pardon me?" the man said.

"You're sitting in my seat," Larry repeated.

The new arrival looked at Larry for a long moment and then slowly got to his feet. The room became quiet. It was a heavy silence, an electric silence, the kind of silence they feature in those E.F. Hutton television commercials. A few minutes later, that silence was explained to us.

"Didn't you know who you were talking to?" someone asked.

"Nope," Larry said.

"That was Joe Colombo."

"Whoa," I said to Larry, "maybe you should've said, 'excuse me' first."

That was the first time I observed the part of Larry's personality that can be abrasive. It also translates as an absolute unwillingness to be intimidated. I still don't know whether it was foolishness or bravery, but he just didn't seem all that impressed by Colombo's gangster ties.

How did Larry Marchiano react to what he saw? Later he would tell me that he knew I was an adult and he didn't feel he was there to sit in judgment on me. I wish it never happened at all, and the only reason I mention it here is to show how confused I was at the time.

While I'm making confessions, I have to admit to one other thing—again as a way of showing my state of mind at the time. This is something I really *hate* to admit. At that time I was using cocaine. Cocaine wasn't just a sometime thing either.

I understand why people get hooked on it. Some people say they use it for sexual reasons, but I found it gave me courage. It was a courage that seemed to translate into energy. It enabled me to get up and do things. It gave me so much false confidence that pretty soon I took to hiding behind it. And without it, I was scared, scared of everything, scared of being alone. With cocaine, the people around me seemed to be my friends; not true friends, but at least there were bodies around me and I wasn't alone.

Cocaine was just coming into its own in Hollywood. Some of the flunkies at Hefner's had discovered they could seduce young girls by using cocaine as bait. The way they would use it was to put it into an emptied neosynepherine bottle along with water. Then while they were watching the movie, they'd give themselves a squirt in the nose every now and then. Often they would do this after they had a regular snort; some of the powder would remain in the nostril and the squirt would wash that down as an added bonus. They would also take the neosynepherine bottle on planes with them, use it whenever they liked, and no one would be the wiser.

Whenever I was taken over to Sammy Davis, Jr.'s house, there would be cocaine *and* amyl nitrites—this was Sammy's big thing. Everything with Sammy always had to be an all-night session and he needed whatever he could get to stay awake. Amyl nitrites—how I hated them! Whenever he shoved one into my nose, I'd hold my breath.

It all seems so ironical. I finally found my freedom, finally got away, and one of the first things I did was walk into the cocaine trap.

A week after my visit to Florida, Larry Marchiano joined me in California. And my new life began.

four

Larry Marchiano came out to Hollywood with his war-drobe of dungarees and T-shirts, with his work boots and casual ways. He wasn't into pornography, showed no interest in kinky sex, didn't do cocaine. And most of all, he seemed to care about me—not me as a product or a sex machine or a potential gold mine, but me as a human being. I hadn't met a man like Larry Marchiano in far too long.

Part of his role would be to offer protection. Here I knew I was in particularly good hands. Larry is not tall but he is muscular; he has always worked with his hands and one of his hobbies has been the martial arts. It was so strange to be with a man with these abilities and never have them directed against me. Larry immediately started cushioning me against other people, forming a barrier between myself and those who wanted to take advantage of me.

And he began to know me, began to realize the kind of person I really was. The truth was this: After breaking away from Charles Traynor, I never again would settle for sex without love. What I wanted—all that I ever wanted—was a lasting, loving relationship.

Although I met many movie stars at Hugh Hefner's Play-boy Mansion West, I never accepted their invitations. I remember the night I met Warren Beatty, *the* Warren Beatty, the same Warren Beatty whose picture was pasted all over my bedroom wall when I was fifteen or sixteen; then, just the thought of him touching my hand would create shivers. Suddenly here he was, the real person, ask-ing me to go home with him. Several different nights he invited me to go off with him. If ever I faced temptation, it was then. Still I never went. It just wasn't my thing. In fact, at the Playboy Mansion I felt most at home with the help, and some evenings I spent the whole night hanging out with them in the kitchen, just talking.

One of the men I responded to was Shel Silverstein, the *Playboy* artist and writer. I can remember just sitting in the jacuzzi with him and talking. I always liked Shel. The thought of having sex with him never crossed my mind; if anything, I feared that. That whole world seemed unreal then and more unreality wasn't what I needed.

And now with Larry joining me on the West Coast, it was back to business. Directly ahead of me lay something I had been dreading—a trip across Canada to publicize the movie *Linda Lovelace for President*.

This was one of the dumbest movies ever made. It was so bad that I can't remember the names of the other so-called actors in the movie, and even if I could I wouldn't embarrass them by repeating that information here. Who knows? Some of them may have even gone on to acting careers.

Anyway, *Linda Lovelace for President* taught me what was meant by the phrase, "exploitation movie." People would be amazed if they saw how a movie like this is actually made. The only smart thing they did was to hire comedian Chuck McCann. The script would go from pointless to inane to ludicrous, and then someone would turn to McCann and say, "Do something funny here—anything at all." Farther into the movie that same someone turned to me and said, "All right, Linda, we're ready for the fucking-and-sucking scenes now." McCann obliged them with gags, because that was his job; I didn't oblige them with sex, because that was no longer my job.

Maybe it was bad enough that I had to appear in the nude. But to me that was a big step up. The movie was R-rated (probably R for Ridiculous) and instead of real sexual perversions, it was filled with simulated sexual perversions. Maybe the audience couldn't tell the difference, but I could.

Not only was the movie an artistic disaster, it provided me with another of life's little embarrassments. There was a screening of the movie in California just before I was to go on tour to publicize it. My mother and father were there; my twenty-year-old niece was there; my sister Jean was there; as was Larry, a man who was becoming increasingly important in my life.

Suddenly there was a picture of me standing in front of a huge American flag, saluting, á la George C. Scott in *Patton*. The major difference between George C. Scott and myself was that he wore a helmet and uniform while I wore a helmet. Just a helmet, nothing more, not a stitch of clothing. Unfortunately, the helmet wasn't large enough to crawl under.

Immediately after the screening, I joined the movie's other "stars." It was just expected of me, just another thing I would do mechanically. I tried to keep a stiff upper lip but this time it wasn't so easy. Larry Marchiano was looking at me with a funny expression on his face.

"What are you thinking?" I asked.

"Oh, I'm just thinking about the movie," he said.

"Yes, but *what* are you thinking about the movie?"

"You really want to know? I was thinking that it's a worthless piece of shit," he said. "It's absolutely ridiculous, unbelievable and terrible."

"Oh, come on, Larry," I said. "Don't be so polite—what did you *really* think?"

It had been so long since someone just told me the truth, simply and directly, that I almost welcomed his comments. However, I didn't really need anyone to tell me what kind of a movie it was. This was not one of the movies where the producers wait anxiously for those early critical notices; this was a take-the-money-and-run movie, the kind of movie you sneak into town and open everywhere at once, before anyone has a chance to write—or read—a review.

five

Unfortunately, my embarrassment was not going to be confined to just that one night. Next on the schedule: a cross-continental tour of Canada to promote the film. And Larry was supposed to go on the tour with me.

"No way," he said. "No way you're going to embarrass yourself by going anywhere for this movie"

"There happens to be a contract—if we don't go, they sue," I said to him, quietly. "And there are 2,500 other reasons to go. They're paying me $2,500, plus expenses. You've been going through my books and you've probably figured out about how much money we have"

"So when do we pack?" he said.

The next day, as a matter of fact. Okay, the bottom line was $2,500 and we decided to make the most of it, to have a good time and not think about what we were doing. God knows I had had enough practice at that—at not thinking about what I was doing.

But I don't think either of us dreamed how important this little publicity trip would turn out to be. Not for the movie and not for my career. But it was then, during an idiotic trip to promote a moronic movie, that we came to realize how much we cared for each other.

For once it was a comfort to have a man with me. A real man, not a male. All I could think of was the contrast between Larry and Chuck Traynor. Say I'd be at a live autograph signing—Larry would check people, watch them, try to stop any trouble before it got started. He was truly protecting me. If it had been Chuck Traynor, he would have been trying to figure out which girl to come on to, which people were into weird sex, how he could cash in on my presence.

In a sense Larry was a fish out of water; the entertainment world would never become his element. In the world of the laboring man there was one way to handle a difficult situation—the direct way. But in my glitzy show-biz world he always had to stop and ask himself what was the proper thing to do. Tact was never his strong suit and this must have been terribly frustrating. At times I could see that frustration bubble up and break through the surface.

Our first concern was costuming. Of course, I was going to wear my movie-star clothes—necklines cut down to my waist. This part of it didn't bother me at all; I had learned that you could get clothes that were sexy and attractive, revealing without being too revealing. At this stage of my life, I may not have known just who I was yet, but I was no one's prisoner. No one was *forcing* me to wear low-cut dresses. I think every woman likes to feel attractive.

Larry, too, had to adjust to the necessities of a publicity tour. In the first place he owned nothing but work clothes, so we had to make a few purchases before leaving. Slacks instead of jeans, shirts instead of T-shirts, shoes instead of boots.

We both sensed (correctly) that I'd never earn another penny from the movie; therefore, this trip—the way we lived and ate and played—was my final paycheck.

Larry got into the swing of things fairly rapidly. Early in the tour the three of us—Larry, my niece, myself—checked into a suite of rooms in a Vancouver hotel. Actually, it was *supposed* to be a suite but there was barely enough room for our suitcases.

When I heard Larry complaining to the hotel manager, I could hardly believe my ears (I had to remind myself that just a couple of weeks earlier he had been an apprentice plumber). Now I heard him saying, "I don't care if this *is* your only available room. Either you find us a better suite or we pack up. But before we go, we'll explain to the press why we're leaving—we're leaving because this hotel couldn't give us proper accommodations."

And *I* was supposed to be the actor! Larry's threat sent the manager scurrying; when he returned he explained the only other suite available was the Howard Hughes suite, the one the billionaire used during his stays in Vancouver.

"Fine, we'll take that," Larry said.

"Are you sure the movie company will pay for it?"

"I *said* we'll take it."

And so it was we wound up in a suite of rooms too large to explore in a single evening. We could have played football in the living room. Since the movie company was also paying for our meals, I dialed room service and ordered the meal that quickly became our staple throughout the tour: shrimp, lobster and champagne, a generous supply of each.

And we sat there, in the middle of the Howard Hughes Suite, basking before a glowing television set—watching ourselves on TV for the first time ever—and dining on a millionaire's picnic. At some point, my niece went off to bed and the next morning Larry Marchiano and I awakened in front of a television test pattern; during that night we became lovers and we have remained lovers ever since.

Getting to know this new man in my life was the only really important thing about the Canadian trip. Every day was divided into two parts. One part was the shabby business of promoting a worthless movie. The other part: getting to really know each other.

Slowly, Larry came to know the kind of woman I *really* was—a one-man woman giving herself completely to the man she loved. The world, on the other hand, saw me as not just a scarlet woman, but *the* scarlet woman. Larry had trouble reconciling the two. I remember being on a television show in Ottawa; a local minister was waggling his finger in my face and lecturing me on morality. There was no way for me to defend appearing in a film of such awesome stupidity; still, I've always hated being lectured to.

"Didn't anyone ever tell you it was bad manners to point your finger at a lady?" I said.

"Who are *you* to talk to me about bad manners?" he

began again. Larry decided he had heard enough of this. From the corner of my eye I could see him wandering about the set; then I saw him bend over to what seemed to be an enormous cable; the last thing I saw was Larry disconnecting an electric plug. The minister was talking into a dead microphone in a suddenly darkened set as Larry and I left.

"I'm not sure you should have done that," I said.

"Really?" he said. "Didn't you think that had gone on long enough?"

But what did Larry really know about me or I about him? There were times when I tried to tell him that I was forced into *Deep Throat*, that I had been the prisoner of a madman. But what happened in the past didn't seem all that important, not when the present was so promising. As a result, I didn't get around to telling him the whole story then. He had never seen *Deep Throat*. He hadn't seen any of my 8-millimeter movies. He had never seen me being raped as public entertainment.

And all he was hearing were interviews in which I seemed not to take it, or anything else, too seriously.

"I'm a comedienne, like Marilyn Monroe," I said in one set speech. "Her problem was that she took being a sex symbol too seriously. Personally, I can't stand hard-core porn films. If they don't have comedy in them, like *Deep Throat* did, I find them boring. They're like medical films."

On a Friday afternoon we were in a Toronto bookstore, The Book Cellar, and I was signing autographs for three hundred people. The manager of the bookstore, Bruce Surtees, seemed upset by the number of people who stood in line for my autograph.

"If we had a thing like this for Will Durant," he said, "nobody would show up."

Although I nodded my head in sympathy, I had no idea who this Will Durant might be or why people should want his autograph. One of the men in line was young, intense, nervous. Larry was keeping a close eye on him as he approached, book in hand, waiting for an autograph.

"Write anything," he said, "as long as it's dirty."

"I don't do that," I said.

"Then write anything at all. I saw your *Deep Throat* film," the young man said. "I saw your *other* movie, and that was really good."

"What other movie was that?" Larry said, coming up suddenly.

"Never mind," I said, "it's really not important."

"No, what was the *name* of the movie?" Larry pressed the young man. "If there's another movie out there, I want to know about it. They probably owe you money on that one as well."

"It was the *dog* movie," the young man said. "There was no name."

"Larry, forget it," I said. "I'll tell you about it later."

Larry was only taking his new job as business manager seriously. He backed off, but I knew he wasn't going to drop the subject. That night we returned to our suite at the Hyatt Regency and had our shrimp, lobster and champagne—but nothing sat well on my stomach. All afternoon I had avoided Larry and now I was unable to meet his eyes. If only he would just forget about it. That had been the worst day of my life and I'd never been able to talk to anyone about it. How could I go over it with the man I was loving? To this day I have trouble pronouncing the word "dog"—I usually spell it out, D-O-G—and I was hoping he would go to sleep and not ask.

"Tell me about it." he said.

"No, Larry. Please."

"You're going to have to someday."

That was my first attempt but it was just too painful. Not that I had any trouble remembering the day with the dog. That day is a wound on my memory. But it was an experience I had never been able to discuss with anyone. Instead

I tried to tell Larry about that part of my life, the time just before *Deep Throat*. We were in New York, flat broke, and Chuck started meeting with people who made 8-millimeter movies for the peep-show trade.

Flashback to—

A filthy loft in Manhattan, sheets draped over the furniture, floors that had never been mopped, a bathroom sink that had never been scrubbed. Two other actors waiting there, a young man named Rob and his wife, Cathy. The director giving us the story line: "All right, Rob, you lie down on that rubber sheet and Cathy, you and Linda come over and piss on him."

Not believing my ears, watching Cathy try to do it in vain, her saying finally, "I just can't." The director announcing, "Well, fine, if you can't be the pisser, you can be the pissee. Cathy, you lie down and Rob, you and Linda piss on her." Insane, so very insane. None of us able to do it and then the director sends out for six-packs of beer. How do you do it, how do you manage to urinate on another human being? I'll tell you how. The director says: "All right, Linda, if you're having such trouble, you get down on the sheet and they'll piss on you." That's how you do it; that's your motivation. Me saying, "Hey, wait a minute, give me another chance." And so the movie is made. Aware of the sickness, the insanity, but still doing it, still urinating on another human being.

"I must have been crazy," I said to Larry.

"Maybe not so crazy," he said. "You'd rather piss on than be pissed upon—that strikes me as a symptom of sanity."

"That was the only kind of choice I'd get in those days."

"And the dog?" Larry said. "What was the choice there?"

"My choice? It was either the dog or death. They had a gun."

"Tell me about it."

"Later," I said. "Someday I'll be able to tell you about that. When I can do that, I'll know I'm over it—that I'm well."

I tried to tell him more about that whole time in my life, about what happened, but the tears finally got in the way of the words. Why even try? Because I had decided that whenever Larry asked me about my past—and whatever he asked me—I'd tell him as much as I could. I knew there was no way to tell it all at once; it would have to come out in dribs and drabs. But in time it *would* all have to come out. There should be no surprises to plague him in the future. But it was hard, so hard, and I wondered whether I would ever come to grips with it.

I've been worried other times with Larry, worried that once he learned all the atrocities I'd been through, he might just get up and leave. But he hasn't, and he didn't on that night. He just wrapped me in his arms and listened as I told him as much as we could handle.

He seemed to react well. I saw him as an antidote to the horror of the past. But I may have been overestimating his strength; I know him better now, and I know this kind of information could rip him apart.

"Chuck Traynor should be killed," he said.

"I wanted him dead," I said, "but I never had the strength to kill him."

"An experience like that didn't give you the strength?"

"Just the opposite," I said. "That day made me weaker, more docile. Now I was totally defeated. There was no humiliation left for me. Now he could do whatever he wanted. It wasn't sick, it was out there somewhere beyond sick."

"It's all in the past," he said. "It's all over now. And it doesn't matter any more. I love you and I'll always love you"

That was what I wanted to hear, *all* I wanted to hear. We were still happy and we would be together. He didn't blame me for anything that had happened—at least on an

intellectual level. Whether he blamed me on a deeper level,
a psychological level, whether his heart ever found me
guilty—that I'll never know for sure.

Throughout the Canadian tour we were able to ignore
the idiocies of my professional life—they were lost in something that was really crucial and important to me. I was
enjoying being with a man. Finally. And just as Larry was
learning about me, I was learning about him.

One incident in Toronto should have revealed more
about Larry than I cared to know. A television appearance
ran longer than expected and we were a half-hour late getting back to the hotel for a scheduled press conference.
Now, in those days the press wasn't liking Linda Lovelace
very much. And when we kept them waiting they became a
pack of snarling animals. Rude, obnoxious, totally negative.
I began the conference by mispronouncing a word and one
of the reporters made fun of that. A minute later they all
started to gang up on me.

In his own world, Larry would have known how to handle this incident. He would have taken direct action.
Because back there in the real world, no one (not even a
syndicated columnist) has the right to publically make
vicious fun of a not-too-well-educated woman (even a
movie star).

Larry was filled with anger and frustration at having to
sit back and do nothing while the press had a field day.
Finally, we were able to leave. Just after entering the eleva-
tor, Larry suddenly punched out at the wall. *Thwaaack!* I
could tell from the sound that he had punched too hard
and, in fact, he did break three bones in his right hand.
Maybe he released some frustration that way—but we
wound up spending the rest of the afternoon in a hospital
emergency room watching Larry's broken hand being
encased in a cast.

Finally the tour was over and we—by this time we were a
unit, not two individuals—went back to California.

"Did you learn anything?" I asked Larry.

"I learned something about you," he said. "That movie was a piece of trash, and you were asked to do some ridiculous things. And even though everyone knows you for things that are even more ridiculous, you came off with such style—I was amazed."

"You didn't mind all that nonsense, all those questions?"

"I can understand it," he said. "Meeting a sports figure, you've got to talk sports. So they meet you, they talk about . . . what they talk about."

"You didn't mind some of the creeps?"

"I've seen creeps before."

"And you didn't mind . . ."

"Hey, I love you."

In other words, the tour was a fantastic success.

six

When Larry Marchiano came into my life, I began to look at things from his point of view. It was a point of view I could trust. Primarily because it was real and so was he. I mean by that that he came from the part of the world—and of my life—that I thought of as real. What attracted me most to Larry when I first met him? It was just that—his reality. In the land of whackos and weirdos, the normal human being shines like a beacon.

Unsurprisingly, Larry had trouble adjusting to life in Hollywood. During those first weeks, as we were falling more deeply in love, he also fell deeper and deeper into my world of lawyers, accountants and business managers.

There was such a contrast between Larry and these men dressed in stripes and monogrammed shirts. However, if he was intimidated by all that polish and sophistication, he didn't show it. I've since learned there's not much that intimidates Larry. He started doing what I should have done from the beginning. Instead of being intimidated, he started asking questions, and waiting for answers.

It had been easier for me not to dwell on such things, to let others take care of business. My energy had gone into escaping Chuck Traynor. Now it was going into starting a new life. I never bothered dealing with the nuts-and-bolts side of the movie star business. It was much easier to float away on a cloud far above such crass matters as collecting debts and paying bills.

But if Larry is anything, he's a nuts-and-bolts person and that's what I needed. Not that this was a one-way street. Just as Larry was able to fill some of my needs, I was able to fill some of his. The kind of work he was now doing was a big step up from being a plumber's apprentice.

Larry asked hard questions of my advisers. How come a former boyfriend had been given a check for $11,000? Why was a publisher allowed to pay only a percentage of the royalties owed me? Why was a river of money flowing toward me and only a trickle reaching my hands. How was it possible to make a six-figure income and have nothing more to show for it than a rented car, a rented house and a peek-a-boo wardrobe? I was embarrassed by how little I knew.

"The thing is this," he told me one night, "you're up to your neck in debt. Just how much I don't know yet."

"But I was told everything had been paid."

"You were told a lot of things."

Larry was not really cut out to be a personal manager. He was too excitable, too easily angered. You can't be that emotional. Especially with lawyers and accountants and reporters—you can't call them names. Larry spent the day talking to the experts and then we spent the evenings trying to make sense out of what they told him. Every hour we spent together made me love him more. There was a force between us, as strong as gravity, always drawing us closer together.

Whenever a new movie offer came in, we would try to make sense of it. But before too long we would realize that it was *Return of Deep Throat* or *Deep Throat Revisited*, or *Deep Throat, Part Three*. In other words, more of the same. And so, for a period of time, I did nothing to make money. Then, one night, after weeks of adding up columns of numbers, Larry had an announcement.

"Do you want to know how much you're worth," he said.

"Why not?"

I was sitting back, relaxed, while Larry paced the floor nervously; I always figured he was worried enough for the two of us.

"Taking everything into consideration," he said, "the money you're owed and the money you still owe, you're worth nothing. Less than nothing. I don't know yet how big the debt is, but it's not small."

This was a conclusion that shocked Larry. He was fresh from that other world, the normal world, a world where people paid bills and saved money and scrambled to stay out of debt. People wonder why I'm so bad with money, why I spend it as soon as I get it. It's because if it stays in one place too long, someone else always takes it away. *Always.* Lawyers are the worst. Some lawyers can't stand the idea of clients accumulating money; when they see that, they figure they're not doing their jobs.

The truth is this: I can't afford to earn money. No wonder I've always hated money and refuse to worry about it. That doesn't matter anyway. Other people worry on my behalf.

Larry helped bring reality back into my life. How did I return the favor? By trying to inject unreality into his. He hadn't been in Hollywood for a month before I was taking him to Gene Shacove for $25 haircuts. But although he joined me on my appointed rounds, Larry remained very much a visitor to Hollywood, never one of its players.

I could tell he didn't much care for my world. And when I saw it through his eyes, I didn't much care for it either. For example, there was a roast for comedian Marty Allen, and Larry was forced to suffer while I went through the endless double-entendres written for the occasion, such as, "Marty called me this afternoon and asked whether I wanted to come and entertain 800 men. My first reaction was, 'Gee, Marty, that's a hard thing to swallow.'"

Possibly because even I was treating my past lightly now, Larry never fully understood just how much I'd gone through. Even when I told him that I had been beaten and threatened, it didn't seem to fully register.

Sometimes, of course, he would notice something amiss. For example, I always try to keep my legs covered up. That's because my legs look like the legs of a very old person or someone suffering from varicose veins. One night Larry asked me what had happened to the veins on my legs.

"Oh, those," I tried to be off-handed about it. "They're going to have to be removed someday."

"Yeah, but why?"

"The thing is, I used to protect myself with my legs. I used to try and protect my chest and stomach by curling up in a ball; then my legs would be the target."

"But how could anyone do this kind of damage?"

"It wasn't easy," I said. "But he was usually wearing those Frye boots. And once he got me down on the floor, he'd kick me or punch me. He would punch me on my legs instead of my face because my legs would be covered up. When he gave me a black eye, people would know. Sometimes he would slap me or choke me, but mostly he would kick my legs because no one would see the marks there."

"God, I had no idea—"

"The choking was the worst," I said. "I still have this feeling about my throat—I can't wear a chain that's too tight or a tutleneck sweater. All I have to do is wear a turtleneck sweater and I begin to feel like I'm passing out. So many times when he was choking me—I would black out. I know it's hard for you to understand all these things, but they—that was my life."

It's one thing to hear a story, quite something else to experience it. I'll give you an example. Just the other day I got a telephone call from a neighbor who had been hearing about pornographic movies for years—but she had never seen one. In her mind a pornographic film would just show two people having sex. That's all she thought pornography was, two adults taking their clothes off and making love to each other. And so she saw nothing so bad about going to her local video-rental shop and taking home three of their X-rated cassettes.

For the first time my friend finally saw—finally *experienced*—pornographic movies. Two of the films starred women who had bruises all over their bodies, just as I had in *Deep Throat*. The third was a so-called "snuff" movie, one where the female star was sexually abused, then apparently killed in a bloody and graphic way.

My friend was in shock when she took the three films back to the store. How could this kind of thing be allowed to go on? She asked the store owner what kind of people would want to see films this violent, this disgusting.

He told her his customers were normal, everyday people and that the "snuff" film happened to be his most popular current offering: "A newspaper said that the woman was actually murdered in that movie and most people can't wait to see that."

My friend will never get over the experience, but now it is just that—an experience—not just something she heard about.

Something like this was going on with Larry. I told him what had happened to me. He listened; he nodded his head in the right places; he agreed that it was a terrible thing; but he was not really *experiencing* it. He was not *feeling* my pain and humiliation and degredation.

At this time I was asked to appear in Florida to be a witness in a trial. A young man named Henry Justice had been accidentally filmed playing Ping-Pong in *Deep Throat*. Justice was suing, claiming that he had been publicly humiliated by his unwitting cameo role in the movie. Since that film had also been a humiliation for me, I felt a kind of kinship with him and agreed to come to the courtroom and testify on his behalf. Justice had sued for a million dollars and was finally awarded $5,000.

If I had known what awaited me in that Miami courtroom I would never have gone. With no warning, the judge ruled that the entire movie, *Deep Throat*, must be screened for the jury. Then he made a second decision. He also decided it was important that I stay in the courtroom and verify that this was, indeed, the film. This meant that Larry—the man I loved, the man I was thinking about spending my life with—would sit there and watch the movie with me. The film he had never seen.

seven

Larry knew a little of what to expect; he knew that he would be watching a film of the woman he loved involved in sex with other men. But he didn't realize he was going to watch the woman he loved performing sexual acrobatics with several strangers.

There was such a risk to this, such a terrible risk. I realized I might lose Larry forever. Some men would never have been able to look me in the eye again. But total honesty has always been important to me. What good is a love if it's built on a lie? In a strange way I wanted—needed—Larry beside me; I couldn't sit in that crowded courtroom totally unprotected.

There was still one other thing in my mind. I wanted Larry to understand. I wanted him to go with me into the very depths of my life, I wanted him to *feel* it.

This happened to be the first time I sat through the entire movie myself. I had been in other places—like Hefner's mansion in California—where the movie was being shown but always, in the past, I would get up and walk out of the room as soon as the lights went off. What I had seen in the past seemed to me incomprehensible, disgusting, embarrassing, smelly.

When it was learned that *Deep Throat* was being screened, that Florida courtroom suddenly filled with people. Every lawyer and judge and legal secretary in the building suddenly found an excuse to visit the courtroom. Although I tried to brace myself, the pain was acute. I sat there, suffering, as once again the rape went on. It was worse than I remembered, worse than I imagined it might be.

I couldn't look at Larry directly. From the corners of my eyes, I could see that he, too, was avoiding looking at the screen. His eyes remained on the floor. However, there was no way to block his ears, no way for him to avoid hearing it.

A few times I tried to make light of it by whispering something to Larry. I tried to adopt an oh-it's-not-all-that-bad attitude but it didn't work. There could never be a way this part of my life could be turned into a joke. Larry seemed tense, frozen in position as if braced against some unseen assault. What was he thinking? What could he be thinking? Was he tough enough for this, tough enough to trust me despite this?

I couldn't guess the answer. As the action on the screen moved on relentlessly, I began to feel spaced out. This should not be happening—but there was no way to stop it.

Unfortunately, Larry was seeing this movie—this dismal chapter of my life—out of context. He, like millions of others, had no idea what was going on when the movie camera was turned off. He hadn't read director Damiano's description of my appearance ("Many times she'd come on the set and be completely black and blue.")

Flashback to—

A Florida motel room, the first day of shooting Deep Throat, *the entire movie crew partying it up in the next room, drinking, smoking pot, carrying on. Chuck turning on me—"You cunt!"—and hitting me. What had I done now? What was wrong? "Your smile," he said. "That fucking smile of yours. You were so busy smiling all day—well, let's see how you smile now. Why don't you smile for me now?" And me knowing the crew can hear every word, can come to my rescue: "First you yell at me because I look too sad, and now you yell at me because I'm smiling too much! Smiling too much! You ought to see a doctor, Chuck, you really ought to. Because you're crazy." Him coming at me then: "I'm not the one who's gonna need a doctor."*

Then the beating. Next door, where the crew is partying, it has gotten as quiet as a tomb. They can hear everything. The first punch sends me crashing onto the bed. Chuck is beserk now, picking me off the bed and throwing me against the wall. I fall to the floor, rolling myself into a tight ball, protecting my stomach and breasts from his boots, screaming, "Stop! Please stop! You're hurting me!" Screaming, "Help! Oh, God, please help me! Someone help me!"

But help does not come and the beating goes on. Why is there no help? Why do the men stay in the next room?

Larry didn't know about this, about the beatings. And there was no way to say anything as the movie played on in that crowded courtroom. We were hemmed in by other people—first the voyeurs who filled the courtroom and then the press vultures who snapped our photographs as we left the courthouse.

Afterwards, finally, quiet.

Neither one of us was able to say anything. Larry had taken everything else so well but this was just too much. There was a long aimless, silent walk along a beach in Key Biscayne, such a beautiful beach, a chance to let the offshore breeze blow away the clouds, but it wasn't working. Nothing helped. Although we were walking hand in hand, I could feel the wall between us. When we returned to our hotel room, I tried rubbing his back. It was all knotted up, as stiff as sheet metal, and it didn't relax as I messaged it. The tension just wouldn't end and the talk wouldn't begin. Somehow, finally, Larry managed to fall asleep. And late that night, when he woke up, I was still staring into his face.

Our eyes met and we smiled. We held each other and we both cried. I started to tell Larry what had really happened and he told me I didn't have to say anything.

We were both realizing the same thing. It wasn't Larry who carried Linda or Linda who carried Larry. It was just Linda and Larry sharing the burden and going on with each other.

Only much, much later were we able to talk about what happened that afternoon.

"Upset?" Larry's voice was as sober as I've ever heard it. "Upset wouldn't describe it."

"You *are* upset."

"Confused," he said. "I've only known you for a short period of my life but that's not you. I was having trouble understanding how anyone could possibly be in that spot. That wasn't you."

And then Larry became angry. Angry with the film-makers, angry with the other actors, angry with the men who bought tickets to watch it, angry with me for letting it happen. And his anger made me angry.

Finally I was able to tell him everything. The beatings, the kickings, the rapings, the animals. I told him what it was like being passed around to truck drivers and salesmen; what it was like having to perform as mechanically as a robot on whomever and whatever; I tried to tell him what caused the fear, the terror of those years.

"You didn't tell me this before," he said.

"I couldn't. I was afraid that you wouldn't understand. I've been telling you a lot—you just haven't been hearing it."

"I can't believe people get away with these things."

Quiet again, much thought. "You know what really bothers me now? That judge, what right did he have to show
that film? And all those people, what right did they have to
be there? Tell me why that courtroom went from empty to
full. Why? I feel like they've all violated our privacy."

"Tell me about it. What do you think I've been feeling
these past few years?"

"I really haven't understood," he said. "Until now."

"I didn't think you even looked at the screen."

"I tried not to. You know what I was doing? I was playing chess on the floor tiles. I was trying to concentrate on
playing chess on floor tiles. But every now and then I
would see something, just a glimpse, and I couldn't believe
my eyes. God, how awful!"

The anger didn't leave him but it wasn't directed at me.
It was directed at the man who had caused the pain.

"I just want to know one thing," he said. "Where's that
son of a bitch now?"

"He's still out there somewhere," I told him, "and he's
still doing what he's always done. Now he has a new victim, but he's back at the same old stand."

"What can we do?"

"We can't do anything," I told him. "Avoid him, stay
away from him."

That was easier said than done. When we returned to
California, Larry went looking for Chuck. He learned that
Chuck hung out at Schwab's drugstore. He stationed himself there and waited. Thank God they didn't meet. It
would have been Larry's sense of outrage against a pistol
or even a submachine gun, and that's an unequal battle at
best.

Larry's outrage came from his basic decency. I knew
Larry Marchiano was the man with whom I could spend
the rest of my life.

eight

Larry never came to grips with the Hollywood scene. He'd show up for meetings with lawyers and accountants, and he'd leave those meetings shaking his head and muttering to himself. If he ever felt overwhelmed by their polish and relative sophistication, he didn't let on. He was there with a specific goal in mind. He was there to ask questions, hard questions, and to get answers, even harder answers. One by one my business advisers disappeared. Finally, Larry and I were left with each other. With each other and very little else.

"I've got some good news and some bad news," he said one night. "Which would you like to hear first?"

"Larry, tell me the bad news."

"Okay; you're roughly $50,000 in debt."

"And you also have some good news?"

"I love you."

"Fifty-thousand dollars in debt?" This time I skipped right by the good news. "How could that happen? I've made an awful lot of money."

"For everyone but yourself," he said.

"But how can that be?"

"Easy—you've been getting screwed by everyone."

"So what else is new?"

Getting screwed by everyone—would those words someday find their way onto my tombstone? I wouldn't be surprised. Being in financial hot water was new to me. It was clear that I had to earn money, a great deal of money, just to keep from going under. Although small economies would not make a dent, we did start by living modestly, eating dinner at home, carefully scrutinizing every offer that came our way.

One offer seemed different from the others. This one came through an acquaintance and it seemed, if not ideal, well, at least all right. The title of the movie was *Laure* and it was to be a French-Italian co-production shot in the Philippines. There would be no nudity and no sex.

The money was good—$10,000 down and $5,000 a weeek. Not just for a one-shot but for a three-picture contract. As an added bonus, we would be flown to Rome to meet the producers and to iron out details. We had positive feelings about the project. No nudity, no sex—this one sounded good.

The movie, unlike many I'd been offered, even came with a screen treatment. On most projects that found their way to me, this would have been an optional extra. There was even a description of my character: "Daughter of the director of the Lance Institute for Pacific Studies. Post-graduate student in Social Ethnology." All *right*! That certainly *sounded* good. So what if I had to look up "ethnology" in a dictionary? The roles I'd played up until then couldn't be looked up in any legitimate reference work.

I started to read the treatment: "Four Europeans arrive at Emelle, an island in the south of the Philippines. . . . These four people have come to Emelle to shoot a documentary film about an unknown tribe. . . ." The film involved some voodoo and some romantic byplay. But basically it was a love story. In fact, I was delighted with the way the first love scene was described: "We do not see them making love, but their actions can be read from the expression on the face of the hotel boy who is watching them from the corridor. . . ." Film-makers I'd worked for in the past did not concern themselves that much with facial expressions or, for that matter, faces.

The fact that I was cast to play a scientist should have given me second thoughts. (Ethnology, as I found out, is "a branch of anthropology that analyzes cultures, especially in regard to their historical development and the similarities and dissimilarities between them.") Okay, that should have made me suspicious. Who, in his right mind, would cast Linda Lovelace as a scientist? An anthropologist, no less. But I was so anxious to be involved in something "respectable" that I didn't bother to ask the questions I should have asked. I needed only reassurance.

"And there won't be any sex or nudity?"

"Not at all," I was told. "The producers know precisely how you feel about this."

And so we flew to Rome to meet the producers and director. That was *their* reason. Our reason was different, slightly more romantic. It was to be together. Sometimes I wonder whether anyone ever had more romantic honeymoons than we did.

Not that it began romantically. That first night in Rome I was in a jet-lag sleep and it happened again. The dream. Once again there was a stranger crawling in through my window. I tried to scream but the sound wouldn't come. As I sat up in bed, I could see the others, five of them, surrounding the bed, staring down at me, closing in on me. This time there was a difference, something new, the roar of lions off in the distance. Sobbing, I woke up in a state of deep panic. Although I was now fully awake and my attackers were gone, the roaring seemed to continue. The next morning I learned our hotel was located near the Rome zoo.

Italy was, at this time, a center for international terrorism; there were helmeted soldiers and jeeps everywhere. It was also a center for labor strife and it seemed that every time we tried to take a shower, the water company went on strike. However, the small refrigerator in our hotel room was filled with complimentary wine and champagne and so we both learned to brush our teeth in champagne; it's not half-bad once you get the knack of it. If we knew what lay directly ahead of us, we might not have been acquiring such expensive habits.

The producers of the movie seemed charming and pleasant enough. One of them owned a winery and he made it his personal project to educate us on the selection of wines. He taught us that you could measure the quality of chianti classico by the small symbol on the label: The rooster is best; the ship is second best; the baby is third best.

The other money people in Rome seemed to be successful businessmen and the director was French. While they spoke constantly of business matters, the conversations were in French or Italian with just an occasional English aside for our benefit. And so while they focused on business, we concentrated on each other and Rome and just having a good time.

Everytime I asked what the movie was about, I was told the same thing: "It's a love story—a beautiful love story." If I pressed for more details, I was told, "Don't worry—we are in the jungle and someone is pregnant and about to have a baby and it is a beautiful love story." I had some trouble remembering whether I was supposed to be an archeologist or an anthropologist—but what did it really matter?

Every day we talked by telephone with Larry's family lawyer back on Long Island. He told us step by step what we should look out for, what we should request, what we should insist on. This attorney—his name is Victor Yannacone—was to become very important in our lives. He may have been overly protective. As a result, I'm sure the producers thought we were a pain in the neck. But we really were babes in the woods, badly in need of guidance from someone.

For the longest time, everything seemed fine. There still wasn't a script I could hold in my hands or any lines of dialogue that I could memorize, but they started fitting me for costumes and that was encouraging. The costumes all seemed legit. Bush clothes, pith helmets, nice white safari jackets that actually had buttons. In fact, I still have some of these clothes in my closet.

nine

From the beginning, Larry pooh-poohed my concern. He took things and people at face value while I withheld judgment. We both had the same modest goals: it would be enough if I could just keep my clothes on and pay off my debts.

There was a single early trouble spot. One of the film executives and his girlfriend suggested a little dinner in our hotel suite. The man was tall, thin, white-haired and dark-bearded. His girlfriend's most noteworthy feature were breasts that were kept perpetually propped up and almost popping out of her dress. The minute the couple came into our room, dressed for action, I sensed trouble. However, we went on to share a pleasant supper and a steady flow of wine.

The four of us had what Larry will always remember as an innocent evening. But that's only because Larry didn't know the codes. I'd been in Hollywood long enough to understand nuances. While neither of our guests spoke much English, they were both fluent in innuendo.

The film executive punctuated every sentence with a small squeeze on my hand or forearm and a meaningful glance. "We must get to *know* each other," he would say. "To work together, we must understand each other's *deepest* secrets," he would say. "There is no reason the four of us shouldn't be able to work things out and get along . . . *beautifully*. After all, we're going to be *living* together in the jungle," he would say.

I knew what was going on because this had once been my assignment—to go to strangers and ignite a spark of sexual interest, in Chuck's words, "to get something going."

And I knew what the film executive meant, even though his words could be taken as friendly and innocuous. Which is just the way Larry took them. But then, he hadn't lived all those years in Hollywood. He didn't know the game.

All we had to do was say something in return, any little expression of interest. These were partying people; one word from us and the games could commence. I knew what they were doing too well. It was so transparent to me that I felt violated. All I could think was: How *dare* they?

"Really?" Larry said later. "How come I didn't see it?"

"Because you haven't had the experience of being around their kind of people. In time you'll be able to spot all sorts of little hints. . . ."

But what they didn't know, and what they were finding out, (undoubtedly to their amazement) was that Linda Lovelace wasn't what they had counted on. Not only wasn't she a slut, she happened to be very much in love. And while all this was swirling around outside of us, Larry and I were in the eye of the storm, enjoying peace and quiet, just being with each other and relishing every minute of it.

Some people wonder how I could come out of my nightmare with Chuck Traynor and be able to feel love again for a man. In recent years I've met abused women who have decided to have nothing to do with men. I can understand their feelings but I feel sorry for them. If that happened to me, then Chuck Traynor would have come out the winner and there was no way I'd let that happen.

There was one other thing I wouldn't let happen. I wasn't going to let that nightmare depress me forever. Larry's family lawyer Victor Yannacone once told me to do a little exercise whenever I was down. He told me to look at myself in the mirror, smile, and repeat to myself: "Hold your head up high and remember you're a lady." I know it's overly simplified; I know it's a form of self-hypnosis or brainwashing—still, simple as it was, it helped. And still does, from time to time.

I began to see myself that way, as a lady. No matter what had happened to me, no matter what the rest of the world thought, I was a lady and should be treated with the same respect as any other lady.

This attitude affected not only the way I looked at myself but the way I looked at lovemaking. I never want love-making to be mechanical or routine—it must be romantic.

To me the act of making love isn't confined to the bedroom. It's sitting and talking and being nice to each other. It's finding out what the other person is worrying about and then trying to ease that worry. It's building up the other person—being supportive.

So I want my husband to hug me when he comes home; I want him to give me a nice hello, to talk with me, not at me. Being together—that's what's important to me. And flowers never hurt, not a bit. It's important that everything be mellow. Because all of this is, to me, part of the act of making love.

Even during the worst time in my life, I knew in my heart that lovemaking was supposed to be a certain way. Chuck Traynor was just an unhappy accident; I ran into him the way a ship runs into an iceberg. It was my good fortune to survive the encounter.

By simply being normal, Larry was able to win my heart. The only part of Larry I didn't like was his temper. True, it was not directed at me, and it was not something I saw too much of in those days.

The preparation for a film is more important in many ways than the shooting itself. Before the actual filming, the basic understandings are reached. I'll admit that Larry and I were being difficult—but always under the advice of our lawyer, and always with the thought of preventing future unpleasantness. I still have all the memos of our meetings with the producers and the directors and they trace a steady downhill story.

During our July trip to Rome, the initial goodwill began to disappear. One of the reasons was surely my unwilling-ness to compromise. A producer's memorandum of an early meeting reflects my repeated insistence on "no nude scenes" as well as my insistence "on the right to destroy any frame that shows any of (my) private parts"—some people have ways of filming other people which make them believe they are in the privacy of their own homes.

My attitude resulted in my being taken off the title role (Laure) and given a lesser role (Natalie). However, I was winning all the early battles. The producers sent me a memo stating specifically, "You are not obliged to play any sex or nudity scenes" and giving me the right to destroy any frames "which might show any sex or nudity involving yourself."

We packed and went from Rome to the Philippines where the shooting was to take place. We arrived in Manila in August. August was chosen, it was explained to me, because the hotel rates were significantly lower than they would be several weeks hence. What they neglected to add was that the weather would be significantly wetter than it would be several weeks hence.

During the off-season in the Philippines, it rains. Not just a little bit and not just now and then; it rains the way it rained on Noah and his ark, non-stop, for weeks at a time.

Every day during our first three weeks in the Philippines, the skies opened up and the rain cascaded down. We sat in our hotel rooms watching Spanish-language television; we viewed news reports that consisted mainly of water rising above the wheels of cars; we read books; we stared at walls. And since the Philippines were under a strict curfew, we went to bed early.

And every morning we woke up and looked out and saw the rain. We understood why the houses are built on stilts. That's all anyone talked about—the rain—and no one talked about it with greater emotion than the moviemakers. For while the rains fell, not a single foot of film was shot. Understandably, everyone got a bit testy.

Our little movie in the Philippines started badly and it soon got worse.

Three weeks later, when the sun first broke through, we were all more than ready to begin shooting. Little did I dream that our first day of shooting was also going to be the last. That first day was spent in developing a system for working with an international crew—each direction had to be delivered in French, Italian, English, Spanish and, for all I know, Latin. A full day was spent repeating a simple sequence—I had to walk down a path to a jeep, then ride off in the jeep. That was it. I didn't have a line to flub (or even learn). And no one asked me to take my clothes off.

Yet.

That night there was a meeting of the film executives in the hallway outside our room. They wanted to tell me about a change in our shooting schedule. Since rain was again predicted for the next day, they were going to do interior shots.

The new scene required just two things: I was to be in bed, nude. And secondly, I was to be masturbating with the lens of a 35-millimeter camera.

"Whoa," I said. "I'm not taking my clothes off."

"What do you mean, you're not taking your clothes off?"

"Just that. I am *not* taking my clothes off!" I said. "And I'm not doing anything else."

This, naturally, had to be translated in several languages—the response in each language was one of consternation.

I was also given script changes. my character (Natalie) joins Desmond and Marcello, and I say to them: "I've seen you on the campus. My name is Natalie. I like you." Desmond replies: "My name is Desmond. He is Marcello. Why do you like us?" I say: "Because you are not afraid."

Marcello asks, "Is there anything we should be afraid of?" And I say, "Yes. You should be afraid of being different from the majority. I know what that means. I also am different. Yet I am not afraid either. Being what I am makes me happy. You, too, are happy. That's why I like you." Desmond says, "You are very beautiful. Marcello and I have a passion for beauty." To which I reply, "I have a passion for love. That's the same thing. Tell me more of your love of beauty and I shall tell you about the beauty of love."

Well, I tried. I read these awful lines, tried to make them sound real, but it was no go. Finally, in despair, I jotted my own comments on the bottom of the script and sent it back: "The dialogue is dumb. . . . Honestly, we are making an interesting and intelligent film, not a fairy tale for children. Which is how the dialogue reads."

Mistake. I guess it's never up to an actress, particularly a former porno star, to comment on the dialogue. Especially when the dialogue has been written by the director. To say the producers were outraged is to understate it. In fact, they insisted I sign a lengthy letter of apology which said, in part:

"The purpose of this letter is to apologize for my . . . comments which I now declare unjustifiable, offensive and grossly irrelevant and which I beg you to consider null and void. I regret my behavior in this connection and I undertake to play the scenes under reference, . . . in the form as was or will be conceived by you. I further undertake to abide by your instructions without any reservations whatsoever when performing my duties as an actress in the role of Natalie in all its implications whatsoever. I shall henceforward refrain from expressing any comments on the scenes and lines I am instructed to play. I shall also accept every amendment you deem appropriate to add to the above mentioned role. Such amendments shall be entirely left to your initiative and decision."

All they wanted was unconditional surrender.

Which I couldn't give them. Because I knew just what their "initiative and decision" would lead to. And I had absolutely no desire to be filmed while masturbating with the lens of a camera.

I was fired. The formal typewritten letter arrived from the producer the next day: "Your comments to the Author and Director are offensive and derogatory and have in fact caused him great stress, up to the point that his personal contact with you has become impossible. . . . Consequently you are herewith notified of termination of our agreements *and you will be no longer required to play in our film, LAURE* . . . All facilities put at your disposal are hereby revoked, and we are advising local Immigration Authorities that you are no longer required for the production. . . ."

In other words: You're fired!

I wrote a letter to explain my position, and as I look at it now, I know it was dictated by our lawyer back home. It spoke of "an outrageous and reprehensible breach of our contract and understanding," and "script changes which have no other purpose but to degrade me as a woman and human being and which are nothing more than ill-disguised references to my past performances," and concluded: "It appears that you intended to threaten and terrorize me into performing scenes which would tend to degrade me as a woman and as a human being."

In other words: You can't fire me, I quit!

Once again I was out of work. Also out of money. Also no longer welcome in the Philippines. A government official appeared to inform us that we had 24 hours in which to leave the country. Not only was I being fired from a sleazy little film outfit, I was being fired from a whole country. I felt, for the first time since getting away from Chuck, both vulnerable and fearful.

Before leaving, I asked the producer to put it in writing that I was being fired because I refused to appear in the nude, which he did with an extra flourish to his signature.

"Linda, I have a new plan." Larry said.

"I'm listening."

"I think what we should do now is get the hell out of here."

"Right," I said.

While we had enough money to get away from the Philippines, we didn't have enough to get all the way back to the mainland. We arrived the next morning in Hawaii with a total of $100 in our pockets and no clear way of making the trip from Hawaii to California. A collect call to a new accountant revealed what we had already guessed: Promised checks from the film company had never arrived.

It took us a couple of days of serious scraping to borrow enough money to afford a plane home. Those few days of being absolutely broke in Hawaii were like sitting through *Coming Attractions*; they gave us a taste of what lay directly ahead. It also revealed that it's one thing to be poor and it's quite another to be both poor and famous. Worse still is to be poor *and* famous *and* a sex symbol.

While in Hawaii we managed to get a couple of hours on the beach in front of our hotel. Also on the beach: an anniversary party for a couple who must've been at least 85 years old. Some of the oldsters started staring at me in a funny way and then I overheard the words *"Deep Throat."*

No one said anything to me directly but they took turns coming over and sneaking a closer look. Talk about raining on my parade. We retreated to our room which was just off the beach, and still they wouldn't leave us alone; we could see them pointing our room out to others, and all afternoon people kept coming up for a closer look.

Why do I make so much of that afternoon? Because at this point everything changed. Maybe it was just a sense of responsibility intruding on a fool's paradise. But suddenly nothing seemed the same. I was broke, unemployed and, oh, yes, one other thing. Wonderfully pregnant.

ten

During our travels my breasts had started to hurt severely. Years earlier Chuck Traynor had had liquid silicone illegally pumped into them and since then the silicone had slipped, settling into no normal patterns, creating unexpected swellings and valleys. As a result, my breasts were no stranger to pain but this pain was new and sharp.

A doctor in California gave me the bad news: I was undoubtedly suffering from cancer of the breasts and he felt certain, moreover, that a biopsy would reveal that both breasts had to be removed. A second opinion, this one from a Manhattan doctor, went this way: "Congratulations. You're pregnant."

So I wasn't losing a breast, I was gaining a baby. To say I was happy is to understate the case. Being a mother had always been my highest aspiration; to be both married and a mother would be even nicer. And that was now the plan.

Not that I ever thought life would be easy. Whatever income we had seen—and I can't recall a time when we had more than $200 in our pocket at one time—came about because I was a "movie star." I put the phrase in quotes because I couldn't take it seriously. In my mind, and the minds of many others, Bette Davis or Susan Hayward were movie stars; Linda Lovelace was a movie freak. I thought about the movies I'd made and there's no way I could consider myself either star or even actress.

And though life was happy, it was also confusing.

Suddenly everyone wanted to subpoena me. My lawyers told me to be wary of men carrying legal documents. Attorneys in Florida ... the movie company in the Philippines ... another movie company in Los Angeles—everyone had legal designs on me. This took a toll on me, and even more of a toll on the man who was to become my husband.

In order to make some sense out of our daily life, Larry had started keeping a diary by talking into a tape recorder. When I go back now and listen to those tapes, I can feel the terrible pressure he was under. This, for example, was an entry just after he learned I was pregnant.

"I hope Linda can put up with me," he said. "I don't know what's what. I draw a blank. I know I'm going in a lot of different directions. I hear we're being sued by film-makers, producers, former partners. I'm warned that the sheriff is coming. . . . This morning I woke up in a hurry because I knew I was goin' somewhere. But then no one told me where I was going."

No one knew. But we knew we had to go somewhere. We had to continue the escape that began when I left Chuck Traynor.

Escape had never been easy.

During the years that Chuck Traynor held me hostage, escape had been impossible. But eventually I *had* to get away. It seemed to me I was running, always running. Running from a sadistic madman; running from gangsters who had, according to printed reports, made $300,000,000 on me; running from the accountants and lawyers and tax people and creditors and prosecutors and everyone else grabbing for a small piece of that very valuable property known as Linda Lovelace; and now, finally, running from a town I thought of as Hollyweird, a town and a business that wanted me to do only one thing: perform perversions in public.

It wasn't easy for a Linda Lovelace to simply vanish. Our escape route took us to Long Island, Larry's childhood home. This was not the Long Island of the movies, not the Gold Coast, not the estates of *The Great Gatsby*, not the storied land of polo ponies and yachts. We were on the run, very much on the run, and our Long Island was a world of basement apartments and lonely out-of-season beach cottages. There was no stopping for us, no rest.

But why Long Island? Why return to a cold winter, a shabby home, unemployment, the certainty of poverty?

There was only one reason and his name was Victor Yannacone.

Yannacone is a lawyer in the town of Patchogue on the South Shore of Long Island. Like his father before him, Victor specializes in workmen's compensation and disability cases. He had represented my husband's family in such cases in the past.

Quite often Victor Yannacone gets himself involved in much larger issues. His real love is public interest law. He was the originator of the Agent Orange cases, the lawyer primarily responsible for all those Vietnam veterans filing cases against the big chemical companies. He's also the lawyer primarily responsible for the banning of DDT throughout this country.

Victor Yannacone specializes in representing people and things who would otherwise not have legal representation. For example, Victor is the one who represented the clams in Long Island's Great South Bay against the polluters.

On occasion Victor tends to be flamboyant. Rather, I should say he *loves* to be flamboyant. And he definitely has a way with words. I was once thumbing through papers in his office and I saw a transcript of one of his typical cases (he was representing Colorado's Florissant Fossil Beds against a group of home developers) and I read his summation to the jury: "Your honor, Florissant Fossil Beds are to geology, paleontology and evolution what the Rosetta Stone was to Egyptology. To sacrifice a 30-million-year-old record, written in the hand of Almighty God, to 30-year mortgages and basements in the A-frame ghettoes of the '70s is like wrapping fish in the Dead Sea Scrolls."

At the end of that case, the courts decided to make the Florissant Fossil Beds a national monument, and it was all Victor's doing.

I first met Victor by accident; I was just tagging along with Larry on a visit to his office. Since Victor had always been a friend of Larry's family, we were introduced. No problem. Victor had never seen an X-rated movie in his life and had no way of knowing who I was. However, since he spends his days looking at accident victims, Victor knew there was something wrong with me.

"Pardon me for being personal, young lady," he said at one point. "But do you have any pains or problems with your breasts?"

I looked over at Larry quickly and he nodded his head.

"Tell him," he said.

"I've been having terrible pains," I said, "How could you tell?"

"Unfortunately, I make my living looking at sick and injured people every day. The . . . ah . . . outlines aren't right. It looks like you've got more than a few lumps there. Did you ever have silicone injections?" "Yes," I said.

"She was forced to," Larry said.

"Well, I'm always reading the medical literature," Victor said. "More and more I've been reading about silicone injections and their cancer potential. That's especially true when they were injections, not implantations. Were these injections?"

"Yes."

Then Victor started asking other questions. As it turned out, the silicone injections were just the beginning of my medical problems. He asked to see my legs, those poor legs that had been treated so badly by Chuck Traynor. They'll never be right again. During that first pregnancy, one leg became swollen until it was nearly twice the size of the other. Two different times I had to be rushed 80 miles to New York Hospital in Manhattan. And today, even though I love the beach, I hate to expose my legs.

"You've got all the signs of thrombal phlebitis in this leg," Victor said. "That requires treatment right away."

During that first day, Victor picked up the phone and began calling doctors. Because of his legal interests, he knew a wide range of specialists. This meant more trips to Manhattan, more treatments, debts. I'll never forget the look on the face of the first doctor who examined my legs.

"My God!" he said. "What happened to *you* ?"

What happened to me, of course, was the awful story I would later tell in *Ordeal*. It was a story I outlined for the doctor. And later for Victor Yannacone.

I told them that a 21-year-old girl named Linda Boreman had made the movie *Deep Throat* under unimaginable duress. The personal prisoner of a sadist, I had been beaten and raped repeatedly over a period of years. I told them I had lived those years in absolute terror, the prisoner of a man who made me perform freakish stunts, who managed my career, who forced me to marry him, who handed me out to celebrities and who turned me into a fear-filled mindless slave.

Victor had never heard anything like it.

"It was so sick," I told Victor. "He loved playing with sex games, seeing how much pain he could inflict."

I hadn't talked about it in a long time. No one else had really believed me and I don't know why I was bothering to go through it again. What reason did I have for feeling that Victor might be different than the others?

"This is a story I can't properly evaluate," Victor said. "It's outside my entire scope of experience. I'm a trial lawyer and I make a living measuring the truth of what people say. However, there's no way I know how to evaluate this. I just can't relate to the things that you're telling me. All I know is that a social, legal and moral wrong has been done to you."

"Can you help her?" Larry asked. "Is there anything we can do?"

"Let me think about it," Victor said.

"Can we put these people in jail? Can we sue anyone?"

"I have to think this thing through," Victor said. "I always tell people if there's a social need that must be met, then there has to be a legal way to meet it. The lawyer's job is to find that way. And, if it can't be found, to invent it. That's why I've always said that legislation is civilization's alternative to revolution."

Nothing happened at once.

Well, that's not quite true. We came to Long Island and Victor and his wife, Carol, became our friends. For a long time they were our only real friends. I got to know Victor well. Dozens of times I heard him tell people, "We're just a small, country law firm"—but that's only half the truth. He is always jetting around the country, dividing his time between his firm's local bread-and-butter cases and cases

involving national social issues. When I think of Victor
Yannacone, I think of a modern-day Don Quixote—a man
looking very much like an unmade bed—always on the run,
dragging a briefcase behind him, racing for one plane or
another.

And this time I was the maiden in distress.

When Larry and I ran out of money, Victor was the one
person we could turn to for help. He sent us money. When
we were at our lowest ebb, in need of food, Victor
somehow showed up with cases of College Inn bouillon
and sacks of flour. Don't ask me why this particular combination. All I know is that there are few memorable meals
you can make of this but you can find a way to survive.
Particularly if you like soup with dumplings.

Neither Victor nor Carol had ever seen an X-rated
movie. When Victor heard the name Linda Lovelace, he
had only the vaguest awareness of who I was. Carol had
never even heard the name before. I don't think my celebrity status hit Victor until one day when he was calling a
Manhattan doctor on my behalf and the doctor was
impressed for all the wrong reasons.

"Victor, this is one case I'd *love* to handle," he said.

"I don't think you understand me," Victor said. "There's
a lady in my office who's obviously in trouble and I just
want somebody to take care of her in a hurry."

Hearing that kind of thing made me trust Victor. I was
impressed by the fact that he didn't suddenly neglect Larry
for his new movie-star client. Which was just as it should
be. Larry, after all, was the client long before I came into
the picture. And Victor seemed to sense that our
situation—total poverty just as our first child was coming
into the world—was taking a severe toll on Larry.

Just how severe none of us yet realized.

eleven

Larry was falling apart. But I wasn't paying attention. Other things filled my mind, such as making preparations for my unborn baby, eating enough and staying warm. If I hadn't been so concerned with these things, I might have noticed the early signs.

Instead, I probably did more harm than good. Larry was becoming obsessed about my life with Chuck. He was asking more questions and seeking more details. I should have recognized this as a form of self-torture. Instead, I answered all his questions candidly and tried to tell him everything that had happened to the former Miss Linda Lovelace. Everything.

My own pain was so strong that I didn't bother measuring the pain this was causing him. One day I found myself describing the little games Chuck devised whenever we went on a long automobile drive.

Flashback to—

A long drive from Florida to Mexico. Car games. Hiking my skirt up, spreading my legs, stopping for gas, Chuck telling the gas jockey: "And, oh, yeah, wouldja please get the windshield." Chuck buying a steady supply of little cinnamon candies—Red Hots—and sticking a handful of them in my vagina just to watch me squirm.

Low in funds. A small town in Arkansas, Chuck pulling over in front of a haberdashery, seeing two salesmen inside, no one else. Chuck saying. "Go in there and speak to the salesmen. Tell them you'll give them a blow job for $10. No, wait, start off with twenty. If they don't go for that, tell them you really need the bread bad so you'll do it for ten. That's ten each."

Chuck talking to himself then about a little detour we were going to make in Juarez. "Wait 'til we get to Juarez," he'd say. "Only 650 miles to Juarez," he'd say. "Once we're in Juarez, we'll be able to pick up some easy money."

Then a new tune. "I hope you like donkeys." Later: "Of course there's no fucking reason you should like donkeys. It's just that it'd be a good thing if you did like donkeys is all. It'd be better for you." Then he starts talking about the big donkey-fucking contests in Juarez: "You're made for this contest. I'm telling you, you'll clean up. Shee-yit, the last chick I brought to Juarez made us three thou and she was nothin'." And still later: "They got the medicos right there. If the bleeding gets too bad, they unstrap the chicks and give them medical assistance right on the spot. Some of those chicks are really hemorrhaging, too." It gets so bad that I thank God when we have a car crash that prevents us from ever getting to Mexico at all.

"How could anyone get any pleasure from *that*?" Larry wanted to know.

"I don't have any idea. The only time Chuck got any pleasure from anything was when it caused someone else a lot of pain."

"Do you realize how sick this is?"

"Of course I realize how sick it is. I realized *then* how sick it was. It was insane. Even more insane than most of the other stuff Chuck made me do. To him this was *normal*. I mean he actually *went* for this stuff."

"I'd like to kill that bastard," Larry decided.

"It's not like he's the only one," I said. "I mean, you got to figure someone is going to pay to see this, someone is going to get turned on by the same sick thing."

"I mean it," Larry said. "I'd really like to kill that bastard."

There was something about his voice, some somber quality that caused me to glance up. His face was rigid as though an effort was required to keep his features in place. I could see uncried tears filling his eyes.

Those days Larry was still keeping a diary by talking into a cassette recorder. This is a tape from that time.

"I need all the help from all the people I can—especially from Linda—to get my feet down on the ground, and be myself, not any other interpretation, and just get things together. . . . I have a young dog. It's an opportunity, at least for me, to identify with certain things. My understanding of the subject states that consistency with the dog—if it's crying, you get up in the middle of the night, find out what it is, and you help the dog.

"But if you assume other responsibilities which make yourself conflicted with knowledge, all right, that's messing with yourself, and doing what you should be doing because you're too tired, you're too worried about too many other things, so you're carrying too heavy a loan and you can't even take care of the simple load that makes you happy and able to carry the whole load. So, I'm upset with myself for short-temperedness in the last couple of days. And I'm gonna mellow out, with the help of my old lady, because I really feel it's important. I'm tired of excuses."

I must have come into the room at that moment because my voice suddenly interrupts his chaotic thoughts with: "*What* are you saying?"

Victor, meanwhile, was considering a series of legal actions on my behalf. He learned the identity of the men behind *Deep Throat*—they were either mobsters or men with mob connections—and he warned us that our lives could now be in real danger. Warnings like these added to Larry's burden. We became as secretive as people in a spy movie, always checking to see whether we were being followed, worried that our phone (when we could afford a phone) might be tapped.

Sometimes all of this seemed silly to me. But I figured Victor knew things we didn't. I knew those mob ties were not at all make-believe. When the FBI ran a nationwide sweep of pornographers, they arrested Lou Peraino, the producer of *Deep Throat*, and one of the men Chuck forced me to have sex with regularly. The FBI identified him at that time as a member of the Colombo mob family.

At the time we were getting calls from a Larry Parrish in Memphis; Parrish was an Assistant US Attorney who was prosecuting the producers of *Deep Throat* for transporting obscene materials across state lines. He wanted us to come to Memphis for the trial and my husband called him in Memphis.

"If Chuck Traynor will be there, Linda will not be there," he said.

"I want Linda here," the prosecutor said. "And if I want her here bad enough, there are always ways we can find her."

That, too, became a cause for concern, someone else to hide out from. There was quite a list by now. It was Victor's notion to launch lawsuits against all those who imprisoned me, had a hand in imprisoning me or profited from my imprisonment. While he prepared these cases, Victor wanted us out of the public eye, out of harm's way.

We went into hiding. We spent two weeks in one dingy motel room, two weeks in another that was even dingier. And then, as the last of our money ran out, we shared the living room of a friend, then the basement of Larry's brother's apartment, finally a rented cottage out in Montauk and a second one in the former whaling village of Port Jefferson.

The very act of going into hiding made the dangers seem real. Today I don't know whether we were in jeopardy from anyone. But it *felt* as though we were. How reclusive were we? We lived in our Port Jefferson home for four months before I first saw the road leading out of town.

The real risk was being recognized. There was always the chance that I would be noticed by the countergirl in the deli, the boy collecting for the newspaper, the fan at a high school basketball game. Recognition—the raised eyebrow, the sudden smile, the sideways glance, the stage whisper—was enought to cause us to pack our bags and run.

Why did we have to move? Let me tell you what would happen after being recognized. Within hours, the first visitors arrive. They might be creeps or degenerates or just curiosity-seekers. But they would drive slowly past the house, stop 50 or 100 feet up the road, sit there with their motors growling, mustering up courage and then . . . finally . . . *doing it.* Walking up to the front door, knocking timidly, and when they got no response, knocking more loudly, as if somehow it was their *right* to be there.

Then would come the cars with the reporters and the photographers, maybe even a television van or two, circling the block, taking pictures of the house, knocking before going on and speaking to the next-door neighbors, the man in the deli, the bartender at the tavern. Asking—and, at the same time, telling—all about Linda Lovelace.

And so we would have to move. Again. Larry would have to give up his job. Again. And we would be forced to go down to the welfare office. Again.

The pressure on Larry was incredible. And of course it changed him. He was becoming a Larry I had never seen before, one I never want to see again. At times it reminded me of one of those science-fiction movies where someone from another planet inhabits the body of the person you love. He was no longer the Larry I had fallen in love with.

I can still play his diary-cassette today and hear the pain in his voice back then:

"We're here for one month. Near the end of September we're supposed to be needed in Florida for litigation. Financial security has been established for our needs through October. November comes time of payment. Which also comes time of new bills. Which also comes time of new lawyers. And a whole lot of other things. I'm back in New York and I'm reminded that I hate it."

twelve

———————————————

Victor's heart was in the right place but everything was far too secretive, too protective. Now Larry took to vanishing for long hours every day. The man who had always been with me when I needed him was gone. And what we had now was not at all the relationship we had before.

One of the saddest aspect of this chapter of our life—let's call it *Escape From Hollyweird*—was that Larry had to take so much abuse, simply because he was married to the woman who was once known as Linda Lovelace. Marchiano has always been a respected name on Eastern Long Island. Once it became known that Larry Marchiano had married the notorious Linda Lovelace, he couldn't walk into a neighborhood bar without taking a ribbing—some of it good-natured, some of it not so good-natured. I had seen my husband's temper in the past. The night he came home with a broken arm after a bar fight, I didn't have to ask whose honor he was defending.

The more serious injuries were internal. The strain of our situation had begun to tell. No longer were we enjoying shrimp and champagne in the grand hotels of Canada; no longer were we hopping to Rome for fun and games. And no longer could we keep the crowds at bay.

Let me tell you how famous people hide out. They hide behind walls of money. Without the money there are no walls, no protection. You are naked and your only defense then is to run. It would have taken a superman to adjust to our new life without some measure of resentment.

What was happening to Larry went beyond resentment. I don't know the exact scientific terms. But I know things weren't at all right with him. Before long, I *hated* Long Island. I remember the day that it struck me—at this time we were awaiting the birth of our first child—that my entire adult life had been spent behind prison bars. For years I had been the prisoner of a sadistic pimp. And now I was the prisoner of circumstance.

During the final months of my pregnancy with our first child, Dominic, we rented a cottage in Montauk on the eastern tip of Long Island. During the summer months, this tourist and fishing village is crowded with the beautiful people who spill over from the Hamptons onto beaches that are a little less manicured. During the winter months there were seagulls and ocean storms and deserted straight highways and loneliness as we hid out, awaiting the birth.

Larry would leave early in the morning and spend the day looking for work or hobnobbing with friends from high-school days. Since we couldn't risk my being recognized, I stayed home. It was then I started drinking. Just beer and wine. That's what I would say to myself: Oh, it's just beer and wine. However, I've never been a half-way person about anything, a person who can do something a little bit and just taper off.

There came a time when I didn't feel the day had begun until I had that first cold beer. The beer became my companion, a friend who would help me block out all the things that made me unhappy. It may have been a measure of my unhappiness. But, whatever the reason, I was able, on occasion, to drink a whole case of beer or a gallon of wine before making dinner. Which is why I finally had to stop cold. I don't drink today and will never drink again.

My only real company those days was my guard dog, Alice, a German Shepherd. Since I had to do something with my time, I taught myself how to cook. When you can spend eight or nine hours putting together a little supper for two people, you can wind up making some pretty exotic creations. Because of all my spare time and my new hobby, Alice started to put on weight.

And now the dream was back in full force. At the end of every day I would close my eyes and return to that rented cottage in California. The window beside my bed would be open and I would hear a small noise there. I would look up to see a man crawling in through my window. A stranger. I would lie there paralyzed with fear, unable to scream, and then I would see the other men, all five of them, surrounding my bed, staring at me. And when I awakened, after the beatings and the rapings, I would be crying uncontrollably and Larry would be rubbing my back and saying, "There, there, it's going to be all right."

But *was* it? Was it ever going to be all right? All of our lives were centered around one fact of life: We must *not* be recognized. We were in hiding. We couldn't even have mail delivered to our home. We took out a post office box in the small village of Belle Terre and since mail would sometimes come there addressed to Linda Lovelace, my arrivals provoked some of the broadest grins imaginable.

Neither of our two children were to be born easily. Because of all those beatings, because of all the abuse my body had taken, I had to visit a specialist in New York City. The very day Dominic was born, Larry came home to find all of our belongings scattered throughout the house. There was an eviction notice posted to our cottage door giving us three days to vacate the premises. Although I'd never revealed my identity, the notice was addressed to "Larry Marchiano and Linda Lovelace."

Although I was depressed, I was nowhere near as depressed as I had once been. After all, I wasn't being abused and I wasn't being beaten and I wasn't being forced to perform sexual acts with strangers. Except in my recurrent nightmare. Eviction? Compared to the past, eviction was a piece of cake. All that was happening to us was poverty. And I knew people could live through poverty.

My son Dominic quickly became everything to me. My existence focused in on him and, to some extent, depended on him. The very first day I had him at home, I must've read him five books. I shared everything with him.

And as Larry spent more and more time on the road, Dominic became my only company. I remember taking a pair of my old blue jeans and carefully cutting them into a pattern for blue jeans for Dominic. Today they're on my young daughter's Cabbage-Patch doll.

A very bad moment came when we were forced to go on welfare. If there had been no baby, I would never have gone through that humiliation. But there was no choice. And on some of the coldest days that winter, Larry and I and the new baby would hitchhike to the welfare office. When the welfare people discovered my true identity—which they did soon enough—they questioned my every statement and took delight in passing me from one office to another for "interviews."

Finally, however, we got some money to live on. We were given a total of $452 a month. I found a house to rent for $250 a month. After paying for the basics—rent, electricity, car insurance, gas, heat and water—we were left with $54, which barely covered milk and diapers for the month.

What really busted our budget was the fact that both Larry and I were smoking at that time. Ridiculous, right? Obviously, we had to give up cigarettes. Nothing could be clearer. Or harder to do. With the kind of pressure we were feeling, it was easier to give up food than cigarettes. So we wound up collecting cigarette butts from ashtrays, bumming from friends, doing everything except, of course, giving them up.

Finally, though poorer than we had ever been in our lives, we at last were able to slow down and rest. Our little rented house was colored several different shades of yellow—canary yellow bricks, yellow stained shingles, yellow painted asphalt siding. The building had been assembled willy-nilly, without any thought or art or even appearance. The roof was coming up in chunks, as if the victim of some malignant disease. If so, the malignant disease was poverty.

In our new neighborhood the laundry was still hung on lines to dry. And leashed to those backyard clotheslines were barking dogs. The arrival of a stranger would set off

an early warning system, barking dogs echoing from one
yard to the next, one block to the next.

Several overstuffed chairs sat in our backyard, arranged
there as if in the Tea Party chapter of *Alice in Wonderland*,
and they had remained there through the heat of summer,
the rains of autumn and now the snows of winter. The
stuffing from the furniture was scattered like tufts of tum-
bleweed around the backyard.

Previous tenants had left tools outside, a shovel here, a
rake there, and by now they were rusted beyond redemp-
tion. There were piles of trash, stacks of wind-downed
branches, broken toys, empty spools used for telephone
wire, a roll of roofing paper, a swing set running to rust.

I walked up to a porch where the floorboards slanted
back and down toward a collection of tiny rooms. The
paint had chipped away from the old windows and now
there were gaps. I wadded up old towels and stuck them in
those gaps to keep the winter out.

thirteen

Without money and without furnishings, we moved into
that little house and the first night we slept on the floor.
Oh, God, that first night! That house was so filthy and we
didn't even have a mattress to put between ourselves and
the floorboards.

Then we started gathering together our furniture, dis-
cards and hand-me-downs. There wasn't a single sofa or
chair that didn't have to be covered with a sheet. The
couches had broken legs and leaky stuffing. The cocktail
table had no top. There was a second-hand bureau of
drawers sitting in the middle of the so-called living room.

Our sole wall decoration then was a magazine picture of Peter Frampton.

Whoever had assembled this ramshackle collection of rooms had also thought to build a small windowed nook just off the kitchen and that became my retreat. I suppose it was originally planned as a dining alcove. I painted this room the brightest yellow I could find and filled it with plants, dozens of green plants hanging down from the ceiling, growing up from the floor and sprouting from table surfaces. By closing my eyes until they were just a slit, I could imagine I was sitting in a far off forest glade, leading a far better life.

We were able to make little improvements. I knew that it would never be my dream home but at least I could make it more than a shack. You'd be surprised to learn what flowers can do. I planted flowers everywhere, inside and out, making sure there would be some during every part of the year. And there was even a huge wooden chest on the porch where Dominic could put his toys at the end of day.

When you're poor, really poor, so much of your life comes down to a car. Ironically, during our first months on Long Island, as the last of our money was disappearing, we were driving . . . a new Bentley, our last tie to Hollyweird.

The Bentley had been leased during the brief period in California when money was a river flowing through our lives. But there's a catch to a car like that. Every small mechanical repair is a major expense; and when you say you can't pay hundreds of dollars for a new windshield wiper or a replacement ashtray, the mechanic looks at the car and you can almost *hear* him thinking: Oh, yeah, sure, tell me about it.

About the only time I remember going for a drive in the Bentley, I was stopped by a cop who wanted to know what a car like this was doing in a run-down neighborhood. Well, whatever it was doing, it wasn't doing it for long. One day we called up the leasing company and told them to come and get their car.

Larry was doing whatever was available, picking up a day's wages here and a day's wages there. We managed to buy an old bomb of an Oldsmobile—it set us back $150 just to get it working, and that was more than the purchase price had been. The car ran a couple of days and sputtered out; when we went looking for the mechanic who had "fixed" it, he had disappeared. That's what I always think of when I think of hard times—cars that don't run and mechanics who do.

Times were bad but they had been worse. Now, when I look back at hard times, I feel we may have needed them. We may have needed the worst trip possible, something to take us down from the California attitudes. We needed to get over the Bentley and all the rest of it.

And let me tell you the major lesson I was learning about poverty: Poverty is easier than brutality. For one thing, poverty has its humorous aspects and brutality does not.

You can imagine how we felt when we went to our Belle Terre post office and found a letter from a Hollywood producer. The producer would say he was surprised I had disappeared from public view. And he felt the public would welcome a chance to see Linda Lovelace return in a brand new movie. And the pay would be incredible; offers ranged between $100,000 and a million. (One offer went to more than a million, this to be deposited in a Swiss bank account.) And all I had to do was what I had done before in *Deep Throat*. What I knew, and they didn't, was that there would have been a major difference this time. This time, no one would have been forcing me. This time, if I acted in a dirty movie, I would be doing it out of need and greed.

And this time I had a choice.

My ambitions and dreams were not lofty ones at all. I wanted my husband Larry to get a job—any old job at all would do just fine, any nine-to-five job that would pay enough money to take us off welfare. I wanted my child—or children, if that should be the case—to live in a warm home and have a chance to go to school without being bothered. I wanted everyone to be warm; Dominic, my baby boy, seemed to be losing the hearing in one of his ears and I thought it might have been because of the cold. When we had to take him to the doctor, the only way we could get there was by hitch-hiking.

A job. A warm home. Kids. Some peace and quiet. Just a few years ago these modest goals seemed way out of reach. And there was one other goal. I wanted Larry to calm down, to go back and be himself again.

It's funny, as I go over my diary, I can see clearly that Larry was falling apart under the pressure. However, maybe even if I'd understood what was happening, I wouldn' have been able to help.

Here's a typical note from that time—

Today is Tuesday. Larry has been drinking constantly and doing his "Humanitarian Act" of helping others. He comes home tired after a couple of beers. He said I was yelling at him. Last night he came home at 9 p.m., left at 10 p.m., not home until 5 a.m. and left at 6 a.m. Sunday he left at 6:30 p.m. and came home at 3:30 a.m. Saturday he left at 11 a.m. and home at 4:30 a.m. A beer each day. A couple today.

What is he avoiding?

He has not slept since last Wednesday and that was only 3:30 a.m. to 7 a.m.

I should have realized Larry was in real trouble. But I was so caught up in the business of day-by-day survival I didn't recognize what was happening before my eyes.

fourteen

There is no doubt that Victor Yannacone has left his mark on the history of our times. He may be one of the most worldly men I've known—but he can also be one of the most näive. On the one hand, I was very impressed by the way he stood up to giant corporations, as he did with the Agent Orange cases and his fight against DDT. On the other hand, he really knew very little about the street world I was fleeing, the world of pimps, prostitution and pornography.

Victor listened patiently to my story but he really wasn't ready to hear it yet. He had trouble believing that people could treat each other so inhumanly. I sensed that Victor was embarrassed (understandably so) to be my attorney. Because he was obviously such a nice man, I spared him many of the uglier details at first. Then Victor told me he had to hear it all—that, in fact, he needed to be educated about the pornographic underworld.

"We plan to sue a lot of people," he told me. "Before we go that far, before we go to that expense, we have to eliminate all doubts."

Victor came up with a plan. He was going to set up "an inquisition." He said that the original Inquisition was a harsh anything-goes trial run by the Catholic Church to determine whether a person had committed heresy or not. I had no idea then that my personal story could add up to any kind of heresy—but now I realize that that word may not be that far off base. And if my story was heresy, then maybe an inquisition wasn't such a bad idea.

Victor didn't tell me much about this inquisition. He just said that he was going to invite some friends over to question me about my past. He didn't tell me when it would be or what it would cover. And he didn't warn me that his "friends" would include some of the toughest prosecuting attorneys on Long Island.

The lawyers who participated did so at no fee. And they agreed to abide by Victor's code of secrecy. While they were also invited to consider participating in any legal actions that came from all this, that wasn't the real reason they went along with it. They saw it as a favor to Victor, part of an adult education program. They were close friends of his and they wanted to help him make up his mind as to whether he should get involved in trying to defend Linda Lovelace in a public courtroom.

Why was this such a big deal? It just was. The minute someone became associated with the name Linda Lovelace, there was a price to be paid. I think of the troubles my husband has had trying to persuade friends and even family that I was an innocent victim—and these are people who know me. Why would a stranger believe my story? And why would a prominent attorney want to get involved in such a thankless and seemingly hopeless cause?

The initial reaction from Victor's lawyer friends was at best skeptical. Some confided to Victor that they felt sorry for him—he was such an innocent, such a babe in the wood. Still, they agreed to participate. As an act of friendship, they would help him to get to the truth of the story. (And maybe, just maybe, like so many others, they didn't mind the opportunity of taking a good close look at a sexual celebrity.)

Since this was several years after I had escaped Traynor, several years since I had stepped off the sexual merry-go-round, how could I remember all that had happened to me in the bad old days? I could remember it because I've never been able to forget it. I'm afraid that's the kind of memory I have—good times disappear in a kind of rosy blur; bad times stay with me forever. I had begun to feel those memories would always be bottled up, that I'd never be allowed to tell the outside world the truth about Linda

Lovelace. Beyond that, I felt no one would ever believe me. After all, few had in the past.

Let me tell you a question that irritates me. People always ask why I didn't tell my story sooner. Why did I wait five years before trying to set the record straight? The answer: Because no one would listen. I tried to tell the truth to a hundred different people on a hundred different occasions; it was shouting into the wind.

There was even an earlier book where I tried to tell the truth. That was entitled *The Intimate Diary of Linda Lovelace* and my co-author knew my story and tried to tell it. The publishers took one look at what he was doing and told him not to waste their time. They said the public didn't want such a bleak story; it wouldn't sell. The book they finally printed made the entire experience seem like fun and games and was, of course, just another packet of lies.

Occasionally I'd be interviewed by newspapermen and the minute I started talking truth was the minute they stopped taking notes. They explained to me that they could never tell my story because the truth presented major libel problems.

One time I even tried to tell the story on television. I was doing a morning show in California, cooking sweet-and-sour chicken, and the host said, "Ah-ha, I always wondered what you'd be like . . . in the kitchen." It was just a harmless little ha-ha but I wasn't in the mood for double entendres. And when the subject of *Deep Throat* came up, I plunged right in.

"Do you really want to know what that was like?" I asked.

"Yes, I really want to know."

"Okay," I said, "I was beaten and I was raped and I was forced—held at gunpoint—to do those things."

"Oh, what've we got here, an exclusive? Is this the first time you've ever told this story in public?"

"Yes, as a matter of fact, it is."

"Well, let's get back to the chicken, shall we?"

Just that suddenly we both became very serious about cooking a chicken. But that's the way the world had always responded to the truth. I had come to feel that it would never let me tell my side of the story. I had learned, the hard way, that the story couldn't be told in books or in newspaper or on television—and so the only ones who learned the truth were those closest to me—husband, family, friends, a neighbor or two. My husband believed me and the others said they did.

One day—it was a Saturday—Victor invited us to stop by his father's original law office in a three-story frame building on a back street of Patchogue. It looked more like a private home than a law office and Victor used it for confidential meetings. Whenever we visited Victor that winter, we also took care of another need. In fact, the first thing Larry and I did on this particular Saturday was dash upstairs and take hot showers. Our hot water never worked and this was, for us, a rare luxury.

A small crowd was waiting for us downstairs. Six lawyers and a psychiatrist were seated in the large main office. One of the attorneys, former Suffolk County prosecutor Jeff Waller, had just returned from a bar mitzvah and was dressed up. The others were wearing their Saturday loafing clothes.

"I told you some friends would be asking you a few questions," Victor said. "Let me introduce them."

Yes, Victor had warned us. He had said I was going to be asked some tough questions by some tough people, but I'd put it out of my mind. Now that the moment was here, I had qualms. I asked Victor if I could speak to him privately.

"Do I really have to go through this?" I asked.

"I thought you *wanted* this," he said. "*You* told me you wanted people to know what happened to you. . . . There are two reasons you've got to do this. First, these people are experts—they'll know whether you're telling the truth or not. I want them to hear the story, the *whole* story. Secondly, we're planning on going after some very big cases—we're going after the doctors who mistreated you, the producers who made fortunes off your slave labor, the lawyers and others who had a hand in imprisoning you. The people here today may play a part in handling the legal side of your cases."

I took a deep breath and straightened up. I resolved to answer any question they might have. Any conceivable question. And as the questions came at me, I did just that.

"Why don't we start with that incident at the Holiday Inn?" Victor began. "That was really the beginning of everything—why don't you tell us what happened that day and don't leave anything out."

"It was a hot day." I closed my eyes, remembered, "Way up in the nineties. I can't stand hot weather. I get the feeling I can't breathe. I was wearing blue jeans, an Indian shirt and sandals. Chuck was wearing his favorite shirt, yellow and black."

"This was *five* years ago," a voice interrupted. "How can you be sure of what you were wearing?"

"I remember everything that happened some days," I said. "On this day I remember it all. Chuck drove us out to the Holiday Inn, the big one near the University of Miami. There was a sign that said there was a buffet luncheon and I thought, 'Oh, it's lunchtime and he's taking me to eat.' I decided to ask him: 'Where are we going? He said, 'To see some people.' All this meant to me: There'd be no buffet lunch because Chuck was meeting some businessmen to try to interest them in one of his deals."

"Had this kind of thing happened to you before?" one of the lawyers asked.

"No, this was the first time. At that moment, I wasn't worried about anything in particular. The night before, Chuck had beaten me up because I wouldn't help run his prostitution business. But here I was in a Holiday Inn. I didn't have a thing on my mind. We walked up to the second floor, all the way down to the last room, and knocked on the door."

"You're sure it was the second floor?"

"Yeah, the second floor. There was one of those little windows beside the door and a man opened the curtain and looked out. There were five men inside, all nicely dressed, all local businessmen, and I waited for Chuck to make his usual pitch. I had no idea what kind of a con Chuck was going to work on them. And then they all . . . they all took turns raping me while Chuck looked on."

I tried to dismiss the whole ugly experience in one quick ugly sentence—but the lawyers were having none of it.

"Let's go back a bit," one of the lawyers said. "Why don't you begin by describing the room?"

"It was a single large room." Oh, God, once again I could see that motel room—I hadn't realized it was going to be this bad. "It's a single large room with two twin-sized beds and a small table in between the beds. At the end of the room, there's a partitioned-off dressing room and bathroom. Right in front of the door there's a small circular table. Two of the men are seated there at the table, having a drink. There are two other men sitting on the edge of the bed and there's one who seems to be the spokesman for the group and he's talking to Chuck."

How was Larry taking this? I glanced at him. He was looking away; I could tell from the set of his jaw that he was angry and becoming angrier. To relieve the tension, he had opened a briefcase and was fingering his set of "noonchucks"—a wooden weapon used in the martial arts. He was playing with them now, clicking them against each other. One of the attorneys knew that they were a deadly weapon and he paused in mid-question for an aside to Larry.

"You know, just possessing those things is a felony," he said.

"Yeah," Larry said, "but I always figured I'd rather do a year in jail than be dumped in a gravesite."

None of us were quite certain what that meant. But there was no misinterpreting the look in Larry's eyes. He was glaring at the lawyers as though they were a bunch of peeping toms. And, I have to admit, it was difficult to conclude that they were on my side when you listened to their questions.

"Miss Lovelace," one of them said, "I was just asking you . . .

"It's *Marchiano*, not Lovelace," Larry interrupted. "It's *Mrs*. Marchiano."

"Larry, you stay out of this," Victor snapped at him. "I mean it. Stay out of it completely!"

"Mrs. Marchiano," the lawyer tried again, "I was just asking you how the men were dressed."

"The men are wearing ties and jackets." I slipped into the present tense because it seemed to be happening all over again. "They all seem to know Chuck; they're very friendly with him."

As I talked to the lawyers, I could remember what each of the men looked like. My heart was pounding violently and my breath came in short bursts. I looked over at Larry; he was under the same kind of strain. Now all I wanted to do was answer the questions as quickly as possible and get out of there.

"What did the men say?" someone asked. "What did they say they were going to do?"

"Not much," I said. "Chuck, he's doing most of the talking. One of them asks me do I want a drink and then he pours me a ginger ale. *Two* ginger ales. Then I go off to the bathroom."

"When did you get the idea that the men planned to . . . uh . . . abuse you sexually?"

"I come out of the bathroom and Chuck has closed off the partition to the rest of the room. He tells me that I'm going to have sex with the five men out there."

"*That's* what he told you?" I was asked. "That's the

language he used? He told you you were going 'to have sex' with—"

"No. You want to know exactly what he said? He says, 'You know those five guys out there, you've got to fuck them all.' I tell him he's crazy and he says, 'I already got their money—you got no choice.' Then he tells me that's my first lesson: "The first thing you always do is get the money. I've taken care of that this time. Now take off your clothes.'

"I tell him no, I'm not going to take off my clothes, and then he's pointing his gun at my head and telling me he's going to kill me."

"You're sure about that?" I was asked. "You're sure that he said he would *kill* you? This is important."

"What he said, exactly, is, 'You're going to take off your clothes, all of your clothes, and then you're going to go out there and fuck those five men. If you don't, I'm gonna shoot you.'"

"You can remember that?"

"I can't forget it. I said he wouldn't dare shoot me with five witnesses in the next room and he says, 'Don't kid yourself. These guys aren't gonna say anything. These guys have wives and families, they're *businessmen*. Do you think any of them are gonna say they were in a hotel room waiting for some prostitute?'"

"And you believed this threat?"

"Yes."

"How did you feel when it was happening?"

"I don't see what that's got to do—" Larry began.

"*Larry!*" Victor silenced him.

"I'm scared, real scared," I answered the question. "I feel dirty . . . lost . . . alone . . . degraded by what is happening. I want the ground to open up so I can fall in and disappear. I'm going through a lot of changes. I think of this time, this moment, and I know it was the turning point. What I should have done, no matter what he was saying, I should've just walked out. He might've shot me—I think he would have—but I should have taken my chances. But I was scared, I was petrified."

How clearly it all returned. Almost as though I were back there again. This phenomenon would repeat itself when I told the stories for the book and, later, for the interviewers. As the words are spoken, the scene comes alive. I do have a strange kind of memory; while I can't remember things I read, I can remember what is said virtually word for word.

fifteen

The bad moments with Chuck—there's never been a way to erase them from my mind. And as I was remembering, the lawyers became quieter. They asked occasional questions—did I remember the names of the five men, their occupations, their exact ages? The horror of that day, the way the five men looked, what they said, what they did—none of that will ever be erased from my mind.

Flashback to—

One man mauling my breasts, then getting on top of me and entering me, no preliminaries whatsoever. A second man, naked, coming over and putting himself into my mouth, just like that, no words, no explanations. Guiding himself into and out of my mouth mechanically. A third man coming over, saying, "Jerk me off, dear." And another man saying, "Don't listen to him, let him jerk himself off—and go on sucking."

Playing musical chairs with my body, busying themselves for a while at one spot and then changing positions. One says, "Let's make a sandwich" and he lies on his back. The others put me on top of him and another man is climbing on my backside. A human sandwich. Starting to whimper and cry, causing one of the men to say, "Oh, lookie here, we must have a new baby here." Eyes tightly closed as they pick me up and move me here and there, spreading my legs this way and that, shoving themselves at me and into me, someone saying, "Hey, let's try to get two in at once."

Going numb then, as if my body belongs to someone else. The voices—"Stick this in your mouth, darling"—come from a great distance. Then, finally, they're gone and the only voice is Chuck's: "You're a fucking mess. Go take a shower."

"After a while, I had no idea what they were doing to me," I said to my inquisitors.

"Did you say anything to the men? Did you ask for help?"

"They *knew*," I said. "I was crying all the time and one of the men wouldn't do anything until the others kidded him into doing it. Another one didn't want to pay because he said I wasn't into it. I was filled with hate then. I was hating not just them but everything. I was wishing I could vanish from the room and from the face of the earth. And then it got to a point where there were no feelings left. Just numbness. My breasts were being mauled and I couldn't even feel it. I felt so filthy, so dirty."

The inquisition carried me from that day in the Holiday Inn to those first days when Chuck forced me into being a prostitute. And with the memories, all the emotions of that time—hatred, hostility, resentment, defeat . . . nothing.

I told them how Chuck made me have sex with his friends—and how badly he beat me when I tried to escape. I remembered the day he said he was going to reward me; we were going to take a little trip to the Bahamas. But, of course, there was no such thing as a boat trip without a payoff.

"Describe the boat to us?" one of the lawyers asked.

"It was a nice boat," I said, then corrected myself. "I

mean, it was a nice *looking* boat. It had an upstairs and a downstairs. Beds and couches and a radio. It had a bathroom and a kitchen, only they didn't call it a kitchen, they called it a galley. Chuck took three girls with him. Me and then there was Sunshine, a girl who was into being a hooker, and a younger girl, she must've been about 15.

"Before we left, Chuck herded the three of us together in the back of the boat. He told us there was going to be a lot of guys on the trip and we should talk to them, and be friendly, but he didn't want us partying. He didn't want us fooling around with them until after we reached the Bahamas.

"But by the time we got out to sea, half of the guys aboard were blitzed. Chuck gave me a new assignment—now I was supposed to set things up. I mean, if a guy was looking over one of the girls, I was supposed to walk over to him and say, 'Okay, if you'd like to be with her, it'll cost you $40. And if you want something special, that's a little extra.'

"On the way over, one of the guys on the boat grabbed me and hugged me. He was a young guy, about 27, black-haired—and suddenly Chuck got enraged. I had to wonder why he was so mad and then suddenly it dawned on me: He was jealous. *Jealous!* That's why he always fixed me up with older guys, never anyone in their 20s or 30s. But no matter how mad Chuck got, he'd never threaten the young guy. No, I was the one he'd punch out later on."

"Describe the kind of guy—be specific—that he'd fix you up with."

"I don't see why anyone has to know something like that," Larry said.

"Larry, shut up!" Victor said.

I wasn't looking at any of the lawyers now, I was staring out into space. But it didn't matter where I looked; the tears in my eyes blurred my vision. I was trying very hard to concentrate on the questions but there was no stopping the memories that came with each answer, ugly memories. I didn't look at the lawyers and I could no longer look at Larry. God, what was *he* feeling? Much of this information was new to him.

"There was one guy who weighed about 350 pounds," I said. "He paid $150 every single week. That was for 30 minutes. He didn't do anything too weird. Chuck made me do this one for two reasons. First, it was a lot of money, more than usual. Second, he knew I'd be revolted by it. But whenever someone was very old or very ugly or very weird, then he'd turn to me and say, 'This one's for you.'"

On and on the questions went. They really hammered at me. And if I was the least bit hazy, they became more intense. They went through it all. The first photo sessions . . . the prostitution . . . the endless beatings . . . the eight-millimeter movie sessions in New York . . . the making of *Deep Throat* . . . the time spent with Sammy Davis . . . with Hugh Hefner. They went through every aspect of my life. At one point I was asked about my role in *Deep Throat*.

"Do you mean you didn't enjoy that a little?" I was asked.

"Enjoy what?" I said. "Which part should I have enjoyed?"

"Well, you were certainly smiling often enough," someone said. "You *looked* like you were happy."

"If you looked a little closer," I snapped, "you would have seen the big black-and-blue marks all over my legs."

"Well, when you were making out with your co-star Harry Reems, you sure *looked* like you were having a good time."

"Let me tell you something," I said, "during the entire time I was Chuck's prisoner—during two years of nothing but sex—I never felt any pleasure. Not one moment of pleasure. Never a single orgasm that whole time."

"But—" the lawyer began.

"Oh, come on now," Larry finally broke in, sounding unusually reasonable. "You people are picking on Linda now. She said she didn't and she didn't. Victor, I'm surprised at this. I don't see where it's necessary. I don't see why she has to suffer this way."

"They ask whatever they want," Victor said. "That's the deal. And listen, Larry, it doesn't really matter what *you* think. We're not running this little show for your benefit. We're trying to do some very serious business here, but we need a little cooperation."

"Serious business? It sounds to me like a bunch of voyeurs . . ."

"Out!" Victor suddenly yelled at Larry. "Larry, I want you out of this room and I want you to stay out of this room."

In dealing with Larry, Victor always plays the role of a Dutch uncle—a very loud Dutch uncle. And Larry usually answers in a slightly louder voice. They can be having what they consider a normal conversation and I'll wish I had volume-control knobs.

"Larry, I want you to stay away from here," Victor was saying. "What's going on here is just too important to screw up."

"Don't you think Linda has had enough abuse?"

"We're only doing one thing," Victor said. "We're making sure she's telling the truth. Otherwise, there's no way we can help her. We've also got to know that she can stand up to this kind of questioning. We're testing her memory and we're also testing her credibility."

"Don't you know enough by now?"

"*I* know enough," he said, "but I don't know whether *they* know enough . . ."

"Well, they better learn enough pretty quick."

"—and that's why we're running roughshod over the rules of evidence. Larry, we've got to find what's going on. There's no judge to protect her here and there's no one— except you—to object to any of the questions. That's why I want you to get out."

"I'm not leaving," Larry said. "There's no way I'm leaving Linda alone with these people."

Larry stayed. I'm not sure that was such a good thing. I couldn't stand seeing how shaken he was, how easily he became enraged. While I was remembering the details, I didn't want to look over at his face. It was too much like that time in the Miami courtroom when we had to sit through *Deep Throat*. I knew there were things coming up that he didn't know, things I didn't want him to hear, not this way, not in front of a roomful of strangers. Although he knew most of my past, he hadn't heard all the details. And that was all these lawyers wanted, details and more details. And although I could understand that they weren't asking these questions to torture me, but to help me, Larry would never understand that.

Once again we went back to the questions. The meeting with Xaviera Hollander . . . the dealings with Florida lawyer Philip J. Mandina . . . the entire sordid story that was later to be told in the book *Ordeal*.

Twice during the interrogation I broke down and cried. I just couldn't help it. Whenever I'm asked about specific moments during those awful years of imprisonment, the tears rush to my eyes. Every time I've talked about that Holiday Inn incident with five men, I've known it was a major turning point in my life. If I had been smarter, I might have found a way to break away.

The other experience that always makes me cry was the incident with the dog, the other turning point, the other moment I should have said no and taken the punishment, whatever that punishment might be. It's odd, but in both instances a gun was used to threaten me. That was the day they brought in an animal. In fact, I insisted that many of the details of that day be cut from *Ordeal*, simply because I didn't want to tell any creeps out there just how it was done.

I still couldn't tell that whole story. But I tried to tell everything else that happened to me. I didn't realize then that I'd have to tell the stories again and again. To a writer.

To a lie detector expert. To television cameras. I'd have to go over the same ugly incidents until it was almost like reciting a set piece in a school play.

I was asked why there had been a constant emphasis on oral sex.

"This is very hard to talk about," I was near tears. "Very hard. Chuck would make me work parties—there might be as many as 15 men there. I was a virgin until I was almost 20 years old. I hadn't had sex with many men at all. I found it very degrading when a man put himself inside of me. I had a choice what to do and I found it easier . . ."

This time I was interrupted by the psychiatrist who addressed his remarks to the attorneys.

"I think perhaps we should all calm down a little," he said. "This is really not germane to the subject."

The session went on for hours with only a couple of breaks. I sensed the lawyers were believing me. Why wouldn't they? I was telling the truth. You could tell a little how they felt by the way the questions changed. At first they came hard and fast, almost brutal, but later they were softer, more sympathetic.

The oldest trial veteran in the room—I was told later he had the ability to make a jury weep on cue—at first assumed I was just a cheap little tramp. Later I was startled to see he was in tears.

There came a time, though, when it was finally too much for Larry to take.

"We're leaving now," he announced. "C'mon, Linda, they have enough information. We're going now."

This time no one protested. Perhaps they did, finally, have enough information. And it was not until late that night that Victor called us to give us the verdict.

"We came up with a consensus," he said. "We've decided that you are either a woman who is telling the truth or you're the world's finest dramatic actress."

Well, I've been called many things in my life, but never *that*. I guess they believed me after all.

sixteen

We were as broke as two people can be. And then, in the middle of our destitution—in November of 1976—there was a sudden, brief, temporarily blinding ray of sunshine. A Las Vegas producer managed to track us down. He wanted me to star in a legitimate play.

His offer demonstrated a certain ignorance of my past theatrical history. Though it was not a widely known fact, I had previously starred in a legitimate play in the city of Philadelphia. This happened after leaving Chuck but before meeting Larry and I had been attempting, against all odds, to be an actress. I had been asked to play a character named Babette Latouche in a bedroom farce called *Pajama Tops* and it was an offer I couldn't refuse.

For the critics there is no happier moment than when a porn star tries to keep her clothes on and play it straight. It's like going to a shooting gallery with a howitzer. Let me illustrate by quoting William B. Collins of the Knight newspapers: "Linda Lovelace, star of the world famous dirty movie *Deep Throat*, has carried out her threat to go on the stage. . . . A whole month of acting lessons has left her a blissful amateur . . ."

There was another review by Jonathan Takiff: "Rarely in my years of playgoing experience have I been so moved—to leave the theater—as last evening at the opening of *Pajama Tops*." Larry Fields of the *Philadelphia Daily News* reported our closing notices: "*Pajama Tops* which brought a new bottom to the American theater—and I don't mean Linda Lovelace's—closed Sunday at the New Locust Theater, a week earlier than scheduled."

What bothered me most about the reviews was their accuracy. You can understand why I was in no great rush

to return to the stage. Weighed against my personal feelings, however, was the need for the Marchiano family to
obtain a square meal, something we hadn't been able to
manage in recent months.

And so when a producer asked me to tour in his new
play, I had only three questions. No, really four. Was there
any nudity? Any sex? Any money? And: When do we
start?

The one question that I never thought of asking was
whether this was going to be a high-quality production or
not. I knew better. I realized that no producer in his right
mind would be hiring a Linda Lovelace to play Joan of Arc
or Ophelia. The most I could hope for was that the script
would carry more double entendres than single entendres. I
was assured that there would be no nudity and no sex, that
there would be nothing beyond double entendres and
innuendoes. And even more important than that, there
would be $2,500 a week.

This meant we couldn't come away with less than
$10,000—and that first month was just the beginning. The
plan was to open at the Aladdin Hotel in Las Vegas and
then tour the show around the country for at least nine
months. Hmmmm. Nine months at $2,500 a week—didn't
that came to *$90,000*? Yes, indeed!

There has never been a safe way for a Linda Lovelace to
travel alone. And so Larry and I arrived in Las Vegas with
our new baby and our meager belongings.

The title of my new play: *My Daughter's Rated X*. While
that kind of a title normally sends shivers down my spine,
the script itself seemed harmless enough—it was an innocent little sex farce that would put no great demands on
either my acting ability or my ethical standards. Besides, I
kept multiplying and remultiplying nine months times four
weeks times $2,500 a week and I kept coming up with:
$90,000.

That windfall would end all of our financial problems.

After weeks of scrounging for cigarette butts, we were suddenly returned to the land of plenty. The Aladdin provided us with a posh two-room suite. It was arranged that all of my old celebrity clothes would be retrieved from storage—it took three long wardrobe racks just to hold the gowns. There was a full-time baby sitter for our infant son.

And the food! Oh, God, the *food*! For months we had been making do with food stamps, flour and bouillon. Now we were back in the Land of the Lobster Tail. One of my first requests was for a microwave oven in my hotel room. That way I could cook fresh food anytime the notion occurred to me, day or night.

Gone were all memories of Long Island. Gone were all images of poverty. And those first two weeks, as the producers handed over the first paychecks—oh, I just knew that everything was finally going to be all right.

And, in fact, there was only one problem with my return trip to show-business: the play closed. To be precise, the play closed exactly one week after we got there. The play that was supposed to tour the country for nine lovely months never made it out of Las Vegas and the two paychecks were not enough to cover our debts or expenses.

The idea of failure and all the predictable bad reviews—that didn't bother me a bit. All that bothered me was being poor once again. The possibility of a return ticket to poverty had never been mentioned, never even been considered, in all of our discussions about the play. How could this have happened? The producers explained it this way: Everyone felt cheated by the fact that Linda Lovelace was wearing clothes.

Their reasoning may not have been entirely wrong. On opening night (shortly before closing night) as I was walking to my room, I was aware of a man following me. All of Victor's warnings came flooding back at me. Who was this? Mafia? Chuck Traynor's man? The FBI? Who?

I came to my door and started fumbling with the key.

The door wouldn't open and suddenly he was right up next to me.

"You've been unfair . . ." he began.

"What're you talking about?" I screamed. "Keep your hands off me."

"You're being unfair to all of your fans," he said. "You have no right not to take your clothes off."

"Leave me alone."

"You heard the lady," Larry suddenly appeared behind him. "Leave her alone. Now."

Larry picked up a folding chair, swung, missed my admirer but sent the chair clattering against concrete steps. Then he chased him down the stairs and away. The scariness came to a quick end. But the man's complaint stayed in my mind. Is that all people ever wanted from me—to take my clothes off? It seemed that way.

Maybe that *was* one reason the play flopped. But an equally important reason had to be the play itself. What kind of a play would have a title like *My Daughter's Rated X*? And what kind of a play would open in Las Vegas? And what kind of a play would star Linda Lovelace?

The answer to these questions is the same: a dumb play.

But still, we needed it. We needed this dumb play just to stay alive. And when it fell through, Larry went beserk.

Part of this collapse had to be due to alcohol. During the previous two years, we hadn't been drinking at all—mostly because we couldn't afford it. When we had been able to afford it, we had enjoyed a few beers and a little wine. But in Las Vegas everything was free—we'd sit down and the drinks would just start arriving. We found ourselves drinking heavily. Each night after appearing in the play—at one or two in the morning—we'd both be wide awake and we'd take a few drinks just to get to sleep.

With the closing of the play, all the old pressures returned. How would we survive? Our first paychecks were all but gone—how would we even get enough gas money to return to Long Island and our life of poverty. My belongings had to go back to storage, a baby sitter had to be paid off and somehow we had to travel across the country.

The very morning we learned the play was to close, something happened that sent Larry spinning. It was just a minor incident in the hotel coffee shop, so minor I never learned the details. All I know is that Larry became angry about some little thing and then blew sky high.

He came to the room and he started shouting incomprehensibly at me. He grabbed me by the arms and shook me and then he pushed me up against a wall. I totally freaked out. I felt as though I were back with Chuck, facing another beating.

"*Get your hands off me!*" I screamed at him. "You're *nuts*! You're going nuts, just get out of here and leave me alone."

When he didn't let go, *I* went nuts, punching him and kicking him. And then I totally lost it, hitting him in the face and clawing at him. For the first time in my life, I was defending myself. It worked. Larry backed away and stared at me as though he were trying to bring me into focus.

Larry was still in an angry daze but at least he let go of me. Then he turned his attention to the furniture. He tore the gowns from their racks and he threw a lamp against the closet door with enough force to break both. Next he broke a dresser and shattered a mirror. Then he hit the wall, managing to do sufficient damage so that we were billed by the hotel for "damages to wall." However, while the wall was broken a little, his hand was broken a lot.

Because of all the noise, someone had called the house detectives and I was never so happy to see anyone in my life. One of the security guards was from Texas—he looked to be seven feet tall and built like a football player. Putting the handcuffs on Larry, he realized that my husband had shattered his hand and he called for a stretcher. Now Larry was in a total daze, glassy-eyed, wandering around like an amnesiac. He looked at the complete shambles of our room and rubbed his eyes with an expression that said very clearly: *Oh, hell, how did this happen?*

Later, at the hospital, he calmed down while the doctor ran a few other tests. The doctor had a question for Larry.

"How long have you been an alcoholic?"

"I'm not an alcoholic," Larry said.

"Really?" the doctor said. "Let me tell you something: I can't even test your blood; there's too much alcohol in it. How much do you drink a day?"

"I only drink beer," Larry said.

"Yes, but how much beer."

"Oh, I don't know, quite a bit but only over the past couple of weeks."

"How much?"

"A case a day."

"A case a day? Well, you may still be a small-time alcoholic but I think you qualify for the general category."

Just recently I heard Larry's tape-recorded diary of that day. This is what he had to say: "The deal was off and Linda had to pack. Oh, God, the stuff she had. So I'm stuck in Vegas with all this shit. All this stuff. Plus the kid. I start to throw a fit. And she throws it right back at me. 'Screw you'—all this. We're having an argument. Suddenly I'm like an asshole. I'm like a stupid person. Yelling and screaming. Security guards coming in the front door, handcuffs, going out with a white sheet over my head—no press please—oh, it was *terrible!*"

The tests eventually were taken and we began to learn the real cost of living with the problems of a Linda Lovelace. It turned out that during our relatively short life together, Larry had managed to develop both an ulcer and a spastic colon; when we finally were able to leave Las Vegas, driving a beat-up second-hand Volkswagen bus, he was on a heavy daily dose of prescription tranquilizers.

That and the car took care of whatever money was left. I was down to my one remaining ace in the hole. Our only source of funds now would be to hock some jewelry I had taken out of storage when I retrieved my gowns. When I took it to the pawn shop, I learned all the original stones had been removed from the jewelry and replaced by paste. A former friend had volunteered to have the jewelry cleaned for me and now I understood why. Not only cleaned but cleaned out.

seventeen

Broke again, on welfare again, back on Long Island again—it was back to square one.

Now that Victor felt my story was the truth, he was left with the question of what to do about it. The planned law suits failed to materialize, primarily because of something known as a statute of limitations. Now Victor had a second plan of attack. I would write a book.

While I knew Victor meant well, my experience with publishers told me it was going to be nowhere as simple as he made it sound. I tried to tell the truth in the past, but no publisher wanted to hear it. The people who had published my two earlier make-believe books felt that the truth was too "downbeat," too "depressing," too "unbelievable."

Publishers wanted only one story—the story of the man-happy, sex-crazed, insatiable Linda Lovelace who knew no greater pleasure in life than offering oral sex to strangers. Unfortunately, that fun-loving, free-spirited, happy-go-lucky sex machine could never possibly exist, except in the minds of a few perpetual adolescents. The story of the real Linda Marchiano, a woman forced to do unspeakable acts against her will, just wouldn't sell.

Victor approached several writers and described the project. To his surprise, but not to mine, he got the same reaction from them that he had first gotten from the lawyers: Victor, how could you be so näive?

Finally, he approached Mike McGrady who worked at *Newsday*, the Long Island newspaper. McGrady's most recent book was the story of trading places with his wife, *The Kitchen Sink Papers—My Life as a Househusband*. At the moment he was writing a syndicated cooking column. I had to wonder what in his background would conceivably prepare him for a story such as mine.

As it turned out, he was no stranger to violence. He had covered the war in Vietnam and a book of his columns, *A Dove in Vietnam*, had won the Overseas Press Club Award for interpretive reporting. Also, he was familiar with American sexual mores. A second book, *Naked Came the Stranger*, was a best-selling group-authored spoof of the Harold Robbins-Jacqueline Susann potboilers. But I guess his most important qualification was that he agreed to meet with me and listen to my story.

During a dinner meeting, Victor outlined the story to the writer: One of his clients, barely surviving on welfare, was hiding out and trying to escape her past as a pornographic movie star. Her name: Linda Lovelace. Although McGrady was less than convinced, two aspects of the story impressed him. One was the result of the recent inquisition in Victor's office. The other factor: Victor revealed that he had recently passed along a seven-figure offer if I would just go back and make one more pornographic movie and that I had turned it down, as I had turned down all the other offers.

The writer's well-known Long Island attorney, Anthony Curto, advised McGrady against involvement. My tale was too unbelievable, too hard to prove, too potentially damaging to his reputation as a reporter. In the days to follow, others would give McGrady similar advice.

However, a meeting was arranged in Victor's Patchogue office. The first thing I did was ask both lawyers to leave the room. They did so—but not without grumbling. However, I had to look at this writer without any distractions. Would he be someone I could trust? Someone I could spend a great deal of time with, someone I could open up to, someone who would get it right?

He began by asking me some general questions and then made a statement: "The one thing that's going to bother people after this story comes out is this: Why didn't you escape? No one will be able to understand why, in the space of two years, you weren't able to call the police or simply run away from this man."

"I couldn't get away because I was a prisoner," I said. "Just as much as if I was in Alcatraz. Chuck Traynor would never let me out of his sight. If I wanted to go to the bathroom, I had to ask permission. If the bathroom had a window, he would stand by the open door and wait for me. He hypnotized me hundreds of times, and if I resisted, he beat me. He often threatened me with a gun. He told me if I tried to get help he would kill my family. If I tried to escape, I'd be dead. I didn't want to die."

I told the story in broad outline and he stopped me here and there to ask a question of a general nature. As I was studying him, he was studying me. In fact, I could tell that he was judging me more than he was judging my story. At one point—I was again talking about being raped by five men in a motel room—he seemed to react very strongly.

"Whoa," I said to him. "You know something, I don't know if you're ready to hear a story like this."

"Don't worry about me," he said. "It's just that it's going to take some getting used to."

He told me not to pull any punches. He said that he'd covered the war in Vietnam, the march on Selma, the police riots in Chicago—he didn't think there was much that would shock him now. So I went through it all, still in general terms—beginning with the day Chuck had me pose for still photographs with another girl, and carrying him through the making of *Deep Throat* and, finally, the escape. And then he had a question, another question I was going to hear over and over again.

"You mean you went through all this sexual stuff and

didn't get any pleasure out of it? None at all?"

"When it was happening, I had tears in my eyes. I felt disgusted and degraded. I was scared to death. I didn't want to do it, not any of it. I *had* to do it. And if I didn't look like I was enjoying it, I'd get beat up. I'd get a kick here and another kick there and then there'd be a gun pointed at my head. And finally it became like this: The faster I did it, the faster I could get it over with. So I learned to look like I was enjoying it so it would come to a quicker end."

I could tell that Mike McGrady began to believe me that first day and I knew we could get along. Later he told me that after more than 20 years as a reporter, he has learned to trust his instincts. His instincts told him that I wasn't lying. Now, after two years and hundreds of hours of tape-recorded talk, he knows I don't tell lies.

Over the next few weeks we met a dozen times and I told my story in greater detail than I ever had before. It was painful but valuable. As I retraced those worst days of my life, I learned things about myself. One thing I learned: it really *wasn't* my fault, any more than a hit-and-run victim can be blamed for his accident. Telling it was a kind of therapy. Each time I dragged up one of the horror stories from my past and looked at it from every angle, I could start to get it out of my system. As our meetings would come to an end, there would be tears in both of our eyes.

Time and time again, I would watch my co-author go into a state of shock as I described one freaky incident or another. Sometimes I'd have to slow down and let it all sink in before going on. There were other times when he would surprise me by roaring with laughter. Generally this would happen when he realized that Linda Lovelace, the queen of all sexual freaks in the eyes of the rest of the world, was in reality just a normal housewife with middle-class aspirations. I'll never forget the way he laughed when we got on the subject of marital infidelity.

"Tell me this," I said to him, "why do so many husbands

feel the need to cheat on their wives? What kind of a country are we living in anyway?"

After a while, the very act of talking felt good. It was the only time I've ever sat down and told the entire story—all of it, all the ugliness, all the brutality. I'm not sure the experience was equally rewarding for my co-author. He later told me that he capped off each of our visits with a trip to a local saloon where he would down a couple of martinis just to get into a better frame of mind before going home.

I found that by talking through an incident, I could get rid of it. Whatever I described, it became less ominous, less important. By going over the details, I could understand better how things had come down and exactly what my role had been.

"Linda," my co-author asked me one day, "why do you want to write this book? Is it just the money?"

"Because I want people to know the truth," I told him. "Because I have a little boy and some day he'll be going to school and he's going to hear stories about his mother. I want him to always know what the truth is."

"And you're sure you want to go through all this?"

"Eventually it all has to come out. The sooner the better."

For the first time nothing stood between me and my past. I was finally discovering what were truly the worst moments in my life. I never knew how much I had been hurt at a sado-masochistic party Chuck took me to until I was forced to relive the experience. I had been so rigid, so protective of some of the worst memories. They had been blocked and now they came out in a flood.

"This girl was a friend of Chuck's," I was remembering. "She was a hooker but she was an 'S & M' hooker. One night he took me over there, You know, just once I'd think he was gonna take me somewhere and see normal people—but that never happened. This hooker was into whips and things. There were stuffed animals, stuffed leather animals, whips and hair blower."

"A hair-blower?"

"I remember a hair-blower on hot."

Oh, God! A single detail like that released a flood of new details; the details caused me to remember what happened, then what was said. And finally what was felt. And by the end of a session describing what I thought was a half-forgotten sado-masochistic party, I'd be crying, in actual physical pain, and my co-author would be in a state of shock.

eighteen

The flashback—

Michelle, her face unnaturally white against the blackness of her throat-high dress. Tall, thin, witch-like, saying: "Linda, we don't want to punish you but whatever we do, it's for your own good." Me, naked, watched by faces white in candlelight. Michelle saying, "Don't be frightened, my darling Linda, this is going to hurt me more than it hurts you."

Tying my hands together, leading me over to a footrest, bending me over a miniature leather elephant, my backside exposed to the rest of the room. Candles flickering against eerie white faces, wall shadows dancing crazily. Then the whip, a short stiff riding crop—tapping against my backside. A hair-dryer, a long-snouted hair dryer blowing warm air on all parts of my body. Setting the switch on hot, the movement of the hair-dryer across my body is slow, so slow. And so begins the ceremony of pain.

Michelle is saying, "And now, my dear Linda, the foreplay is coming to an end. You must prepare yourself for the . . . ah . . . true punishment," Producing a dildo. "I only wish you were a man, not a girl. I wouldn't do this to a girl unless she had been very *naughty."*

Prodding me with the dildo, working it into my rectum. I begin screaming but she does not slow down. Candlelight glistening off the perspiration on Chuck's face, a face now coming alive with pleasure. Michelle stabbing into me faster and faster, harder and harder. The most intense pain I've ever known. "Oh, God! Stop her! Make her stop! She's killing me!" Michelle is sobbing out her breaths now; both hands on the dildo as she stabs it into me over and over again. The warmth of blood gushing out from me, the room spinning slowly around me.

"These people were so sick—all except one man," I was saying. "There I was, bleeding profusely, and all I heard were people saying, 'More! More!' And then I heard the voice of the one sane person and he was saying, 'Hey, aren't you guys getting a little carried away?' Then I heard him say, 'This is too far out for me.' If it hadn't been for him, they might have gone on until I was dead."

Telling the stories was never automatic, never simple. At times it was impossible. There are memories that run so deep in me that I cannot pry them loose. And then we were coming to that darkest day, the day Chuck forced me to submit to a dog for an 8-millimeter movie. I don't remember how much money Chuck picked up for that— $150, if he was lucky. What he purchased for that was my worst nightmare.

There was snow in the forecast the day we were to talk about that. It was gray and heavy, a perfect match for my mood. The questions went on, just as on any other day: What happened next? What did he say then? What did they do with the animal next? What *kind* of dog was it? Oh, I was trying—I was trying so hard—but I just couldn't. My responses were different on this day. Each question opened a wound and it was all I could do to get out a monosyllabic answer—just "Yes" or "No." Then it became, "I don't remember."

"Stop," I finally said. "Please, stop. Why does this have to go in the book?"

"Because we're putting everything in—that's what we agreed."

"But why this?"

"Because this book is an attack on people who have mistreated you. We're explaining how you were terrorized, how you were forced to do everything that you did. This is crucial, the moment of greatest terror, the most degrading thing that ever happened to you. Why on earth would we *not* have this?"

"Because it's too awful, too horrible! I don't want anyone to read about it. I don't want my family to know."

"It'll be no worse to them than all the other things."

"It's worse," I said.

But he continued with the questions, continued until they just became too much for me. There came a time when I stopped answering. He brought me back too far, too clearly, and I was there again, there in that dungeon with the three men, the gun, the dog, the fear. I froze.

"Is something the matter?" my co-author asked. "What *is* that matter?"

"What do you mean?"

"You're looking at me like you hate me," he said. "You look like you'd like to kill me."

"No," I said. "I want to stop here. Let's stop now."

"But—"

"No, really. It's better we stop here."

It was not just Mike I was hating—it was *all* men. The nightmare had become too real and he was there so he was part of it. He was right. I had been hating him just as I had been hating everyone connected with that moment, with that part of my life. And we ended the session then—a little bit early, but just in time, as far as I was concerned.

On subsequent afternoons Mike tried to get back to that incident, but I had said all that I was going to say. It took too much of a toll. And, in fact, when *Ordeal* came out, I managed to omit that scene. I wish I could have erased it as easily from my life and from my memory. It was the only part of the book that was softened, blurred, made more fit for human consumption. I still can't stand the thought of people going through that degredation with me.

Just as Mike had trouble getting over our talks, so did I.

At this point, as *Ordeal* was being written, Larry and I were at our lowest ebb. We were totally dependent on welfare. Carol, Victor's wife, was a former nurse, so whenever Dominic got sick, I'd call her and ask what to do. At times she came over and took me out shopping for groceries. She'd always bring a little present for Dominic. Or she'd bring us things that couldn't be purchased with foods stamps—like dog biscuits for our dog Alice. It was a good thing that Carol was a pet lover or our dog might not have made it through the hard times.

The writing of *Ordeal* proved as much a strain on Larry as it did on me. After every working session with Mike, Larry would sit down and begin the third degree. What had we talked about that day? What happened? Was I going to be involved in another pornographic book or would we be taking a more psychological approach?

Larry wasn't trusting anyone these days. Something was going on with him that I didn't understand at all. One morning he was driving me to an interview session when he became convinced that we were being followed by three men in a dark sedan. I looked back and saw nothing suspicious, just three men apparently on their way to work. Who were they?

"I know who they are," Larry said. "They don't fool me."

"Larry, who are they?"

"They've been following us for the past three days," he said. "Last night when we were down at the dock, they were down there, too."

"I didn't see—"

"They were in a pickup truck," he said. "One of them was wearing a beard."

"But who are they?"

"Mafia," he said. "That much I know. Hang on, here we go. We're gonna lose those dudes."

Larry doesn't even remember this incident today. I'll never forget it. Larry had cracked. He was convinced that the three men were figures from my violent past—pornographers, mobsters, sexual deviates. As I looked at Larry more closely, I could see how upset he was.

The escape route he chose was a treacherous one. He raced the car through suburban shopping centers, bounced wildly over curbs, ran through red lights, narrowly missed a head-on collision with a school bus and almost managed to kill us several times during our "escape."

Finally, I couldn't take it any more. Larry needed professional help and we both knew it. There were two emotional breakdowns, two episodes he doesn't want me to write about, and I'll honor his wish. However, he was fortunate enough to find a psychiatrist who soon figured out that Larry was the victim of a chemical imbalance. The drug, lithium, seemed to help. It calmed him down, smoothed out the highs and lows, made it possible for Larry to live with himself and therefore for us to live together and survive.

It took considerable time before Larry would trust anybody. Because of his precarious state, he had agreed that it would be a bad idea for him to read any of the manuscript of *Ordeal*. It was bad enough that I was reliving the time with Chuck; it would serve no good to drag Larry into it.

However, one night he happened to come across a single page of the manuscript, a page detailing a typical sexual humiliation. Although it was nearly one o'clock in the morning, I could hear him on the telephone, shouting at my co-author: "I don't want you talking to my wife ever again. I've just read a page of your book and you're trying to involve my wife in another dirty book. I won't have it!"

So saying, he slammed down the telephone. And what my co-author was hearing that night, I heard every night. This incident was more an example of my husband's rigidity than any emotional problems he was having at the time. Larry is amazingly puritanical in many respects. I say "amazingly" because he has always operated in a rough world. Most of his life he has been a laborer; he can install cable television systems, run a junk yard or spackle an apartment building. Yet, he won't look at a copy of *Playboy* magazine. I'm sure he's never been unfaithful to me, and he simply did not want our book to carry the kind of details that it did. Understanding his nature, I'd made a deal with him at the beginning: I would write the book but only if he agreed never to read it. The only time he violated our agreement was the night he called Mike McGrady.

Larry has never seen an X-rated movie, except for the few moments of *Deep Throat* that could not be avoided in the Miami courtroom. If an R-rated movie on closed-circuit television has so much as a single nude scene, he'll get up and change the channel. Let me tell you a typical experience. One night we went with our good friends, Danny and Gwen, to see a movie that had received some excellent reviews. This was *Midnight Express*, the story of a young man who was arrested trying to smuggle drugs out of Turkey.

Halfway through the movie, there's a scene where the hero, locked up in a Turkish prison, is visited by his girlfriend. They're separated by a glass partition but the girl takes off her shirt so that he can once again see her breasts.

Even this was too much for Larry. It was a highly dramatic moment and the movie theater was hushed. Except for my husband. All of a sudden, I heard him say, "Awwww, no, I can't believe it, here we go again." And then, when everyone around him started making "ssssh" noises, he got to his feet and went out to buy popcorn.

But that's one of the reasons I've loved my husband. Because he's different from other men. If Larry's out working with a crew installing cable and it starts to rain, quite often they'll all pile into a topless bar for a brew while Larry sits in the truck reading a newspaper.

I may be prudish myself—I guess I am—but nothing like my husband. If Larry's not at home, I'll go so far as to watch an R-rated movie on cable. But if he's with me, I won't. I hate it when they take sex and just throw it into a story where it doesn't belong naturally. It seems to me that movies have gotten very trashy this way. And there are times when I'll get just as aggravated as my husband.

This may seem a bit unreal to you if you've read all of *Ordeal*. But that was the toughest decision we had to make in writing that book—what to put in and what to leave out. The last thing I wanted to hear was that I had written a pornographic book myself.

Our major problem was to get people to believe my story. The best way to do this, we decided, was to tell it all. It was a hard decision, but we decided not to prettify any part of the book. That meant the language would be as harsh as the scenes we were describing. It also meant we wouldn't change the names of anyone, not the Hollywood superstars or the mobsters or the corrupt doctors and lawyers.

The important thing was that the truth be told. Since school days I've believed that a greater judge will judge those who lie and I still believe that. The book *Ordeal* would be my one chance to get the truth out and I wasn't about to tamper with it. That way, when people read the story and experienced in some way what I went through— all the horrible details, all the names, all the facts, all the terror—they'd have to know that someone couldn't sit down and make it up.

After our first sessions, there was enough tape-recorded material for Mike to put together a presentation—an outline and sample chapter. A prominent agent sent this to leading publishers. My co-author told me not to worry about a thing. He pointed out that the book had more sex and violence—none of it gratuitous—than any other book around. It had a sprinkling of famous names. It featured the Mafia. It said a great deal about America and what had been going on in our country. He said this was one book that couldn't miss.

"I once heard writing defined as 'turning one's worst moments into money,'" he explained. "Never has anyone had so many worst moments. Never will writers make so much money."

Wrong.

A year would go by before we would get together again. During that time, 33 publishers were offered the opportunity to publish *Ordeal*. Mike told me that never before had he received such rapid and emphatic turndowns. I got a chance to read some of the rejection letters and I could tell that the publishers had not read the outline, had in fact not gotten much beyond the name Linda Lovelace. They clearly ranked the name (as did most people of intelligence) about midway between Adolf Hitler and Lucretia Borgia in appeal. The publishers wrote that Linda Lovelace was "old hat," that she had been "out of the limelight for too many moons now," that "everyone here wonders why she hasn't made more movies lately."

One leading publisher told Mike not to "bother me with any more of these peripheral little projects." Two of the publishers decided that the story was "depressing" and "downbeat." However, they might be interested if I would try my hand at a how-to book, as in *How to Please a Man*.

I guess even publishers can miss the point. But this didn't surprise me as much as it did Mike. I already knew that publishers, like the rest of the world, were so anxious to buy the lie—to believe that Linda Lovelace was a willing participant and sexual freak—that they couldn't hear the truth. And the few publishers who did understand the premise were too scared. Either people would find it "unbelievable" or it would prove "libelous."

About this time, I began to wonder how anyone ever managed to get the truth told in this country. I still do. It isn't easy.

By this time, the agent had given up on the book. Mike decided to take it to an old friend, publisher Lyle Stuart. Lyle is the gadfly of the publishing world, a courageous maverick who believes in his own judgment, and always does things his way. Mike and Lyle had done one book together previously—the best-selling spoof, *Naked Came The Stranger*.

Lyle immediately recognized the possibilities in my story and agreed to publish it *if* it was true. He gave it the name *Ordeal*. So finally we had a publisher, and we were able to go over the story in fine detail one last time. Mike looked upon this as the final test. By comparing the original tapes with the later tapes, he was able to compare my recollections. He found that while my wording changed, none of the details varied from one telling to the next. It wasn't memorized and it wasn't fabricated. He was sure I was telling the truth.

And along the way, Mike learned what kind of a person I am—really am—not at all the kind of person the world saw. He learned that I'm not the kind of person who would willingly sit through *Deep Throat*, let alone star in it.

I guess I'm the kind of person you would expect from the daughter of a cop, a graduate of Catholic schools, a person who once wanted to be a nun, and now only wanted a happy family. The kind of person who liked nothing better than sitting around the house on a Saturday afternoon, having a few beers and watching the football game with her husband.

And later Mike was able to put that person—Linda Marchiano, not Linda Lovelace—into a book.

And Lyle Stuart put a cover on it.

We were ready.

Now, the test.

Could we change the world's mind?

nineteen

Thank God for time. Eight years had passed since the making of *Deep Throat*. At least five years had passed since I escaped Chuck Traynor. It had been three years since I last saw a Hollywood producer. And now, at long last, after all this time, a few people believed me.

Victor Yannacone believed me, as did the other lawyers who had met to quiz me. A writer believed me and a publisher believed me. That just left the rest of the world.

How could I convince the rest of the world? What would you do if it were desperately important to convince people that you were telling the truth? Often people will say, "If you don't believe me, I'll take a lie-detector test." Of course, not many people are prepared to go that far. I was. It was something I'd talked about in the past, something I'd thought about and something I was prepared to do.

When the idea of a lie-detector test first came up it didn't bother me in the least. After all, *I* knew I was telling the truth. And I realized that an official lie-detector test might put a lot of other minds to rest. After all, some fairly important people were risking their reputations and a great many dollars on the assumption that I was telling the truth.

Our deal with Lyle Stuart required that I pass the test and pay for it. The lie detector expert that the lawyers recommended was Natale—"Nat"—Laurendi. He was going to be expensive, but everyone said he was the best. Newspaperman Jimmy Breslin has described him as "the top name in the field in this town." A policeman for 24 years, Nat Laurendi was New York City's Chief Polygraphist from 1961 to 1975. Famous for his work in the gory Wylie-Hoffert "career girls" murder case, he's the one they call on in the biggest murder cases.

After two grueling days in Nat Laurendi's offices in lower Manhattan, I trusted him completely. He is big and gruff with a strong New York accent. He still looks like the cop he once was, and I knew he was nobody's pushover. When we met he told me he'd read my manuscript over the weekend. He didn't say whether he liked it or not or whether he believed it or not—but we both knew that his opinion wasn't really important. What mattered now, *all* that mattered, was whether his machine believed me or not.

It seemed so strange that my fate would rest in the hands of a machine. Actually, not the hands so much as the arms—mechanical arms that held pens that traced patterns over graph paper. As Laurendi introduced me to the equipment, he described it in technical detail, calling in a four-pen Stoelting 22695 desk model polygraph. To me it was just another machine.

Laurendi had gone through the galleys of the book and had then familiarized himself with 114 questions supplied by my co-author. Those questions were designed to cover every potentially libelous point in the book. There were also 12 general questions designed to determine whether I had been honest in my overall view of the story.

As Laurendi strapped me into the chair and carefully wired my fingers to the machine, he carried on a conversation about the book. I couldn't tell whether he was striving for information or just trying to put me at ease.

"Your co-author, this Mike McGrady, did you lie to him?" he asked.

"I didn't lie to him."

"Not one little teensy bit? Everything you say here is the . . ."

". . . the absolute truth."

"Not even one little tiny white lie?"

"No."

"Before we go into detail on certain situations, I want to make sure there is no evidence contrary to what you state here. Now remember, I read the book."

"No, it's all true."

"You didn't draw on your . . . ah . . . creative writing abilities to . . . ah . . . embellish certain scenes?"

"No."

"You didn't use a little imagination?"

"No."

"This is the simple truth then? I want you to know we're going into every page of the book."

"That's all right. I'm ready for it."

That was my only lie to Nat Laurendi. The truth was this: I was *more* than ready, I was *anxious*. This was my chance to clear my reputation. This was the story I had been trying to tell for the better part of a decade. If the only way I could get my story told was to tell it to a machine, then so be it; that's what I would do.

How anxious was I? Reaching Laurendi's office cost me personally a total of $2,500—$1,300 for him and $1,200 in lawyer's fees. That added up to half of my advance for the book. Now, several years later, I consider the money that went to Laurendi one of the best investments I've ever made.

Although a lie detector test is not considered hard evidence in a court of law, it has its uses. When a man is as well known and trusted as Nat Laurendi, he is often called as an expert witness and he testifies about his opinions. And, in fact, Nat Laurendi has already been summoned to give testimony about the polygraph test we took during those two days.

No one is more aware of the machine's limitations than Laurendi himself. He gave me a printed statement of his that sums it up: "The polygraph is an excellent interrogative and investigative tool. It is not an automatic, modern, technical shortcut to determine truth or deception. It is not the final arbiter as to guilt or innocence. It does not give a printout like a computer card. No one 'passes' or 'flunks' a lie detector test. . . . When the results are made known to the public or to the press that a person 'passed' a lie detector test, it must be made known to what specific questions was the person being truthful. Sometimes a person 'passes' a test without any relevant questions being asked. This is called skirting the issue. A person can 'pass' certain questions and 'flunk' other questions on the same test."

There was no way for us to skirt the issue or to limit ourselves just to safe questions. There were too many people concerned about the outcome of this test and they all suggested questions. These included the lawyers, the publisher and a co-author who was about to learn whether he'd just thrown away a year's work or not. I think they were all surprised by my own lack of nervousness. I have to wonder whether they really believed me as completely as they claimed to.

And so the official questions began, questions that all referred to specific sections of the book.

"Were you known as 'Miss Holy Holy' in grade school and did you really want to be a nun?"

And: "Did Chuck Traynor urge you to help him run his prostitution business?"

And: "Did beating you excite Chuck sexually?"

And: "Did Chuck Traynor point a gun at you and force you to have sex with five men in a motel room?"

And: "Did you see a gun on the set of the dog movie?"

Through most of it, I remained cool and collected. I had been able to consider the questions calmly and answer them in a steady voice. Why does this particular subject have to keep coming up and why do I always have to respond the way that I do? Suddenly I was in tears. Nat Laurendi took a break for a few minutes, then proceeded. Except for softening his tone of voice slightly, he showed no reaction to my tears.

To him the test was everything. His eyes seldom left the different needles scratching out lines on sheets of paper. As he moved on to the primary questions, his voice became a monotone.

"Did all the things you describe in your manuscript actually happen to you?"

"Yes," I said.

A pause. Then—

"Were you forced by Chuck Traynor to have sex with five guys in South Miami, Florida in 1971?"

"Yes."

Another pause. And then again, two questions about dogs—first the dog in the 8-millimeter movie, then the dog that *Playboy* publisher Hugh Hefner wanted me to have sex with.

"Did you tell the truth about the incidents involving the two dogs?"

Oh, *God*! I could hardly talk. Did they think I was making *that* up? Why would anyone lie about an experience like that? Waves of disgust passed over me, silencing any response I might have made to the question, but registering small peaks of emotion on the charts.

How that moment would be analyzed! In the final polygraphic report Laurendi prepared for the lawyers, he described it this way: "There were highly emotional reactions following the question [about the dogs], specifically a blood pressure rise, sweat gland activity and in the breathing patterns. During the asking of the question . . . there were strong reactions in both pneumographic reading tracings and a violent and dramatic blood pressure rise to that question.

"It is my professional opinion that Subject was answering truthfully [but] because of the dramatic reaction to question number four which was followed by Subject crying, no opinion could be given.

"However, writer is convinced that Subject was not attempting deception. Since she broke down and cried, writer did not deem it proper or wise to examine her further on the polygraph."

Of the 114 less important questions, only one gave me trouble. For the life of me, I couldn't understand why.

Part of my manuscript described a long-standing sexual relationship with a Hollywood star. At one point in the book I off-handedly mentioned that the Hollywood star's wife would then have sex with Chuck Traynor. When I was asked whether that was true, I said "Yes." But the needles must have registered something out of the ordinary because suddenly Laurendi was pressing me on it.

His additional questions led to the explanation. The truth is that I would wander off with the Hollywood star, leaving his wife to entertain Chuck. And while I *assumed* they had sex together, I had never actually witnessed it. And since I didn't *know* it to be a fact, the needles registered my uncertainty. As a result, the whole section about her was removed from the book.

Of the 114 questions, that was the only one to raise a small flag of doubt.

But it was by no means my only bad moment. There were many times when Laurendi had to guide me through sudden squalls of tears. Still, he never gave up, never lost sight of his goal. He always managed to get back to the questions and hammer away at them until he was satisfied that he had an accurate reading.

Once I cried after an innocuous question, this time a question that had to do with my father's relationship with my mother. This time I came near breaking down altogether and this time Laurendi assumed an almost fatherly tone in talking to me.

"Hey, take it easy now," he said. "Pretty soon it will be all over."

"I know, I know. I was just thinking of something else. I'm pretty emotional because last night I was watching a movie on Home Box Office, *Hard Core*, where George C. Scott searches and searches for his daughter. Why didn't my father look for me?"

"Your father didn't go lookin for you?"

"No. And he saw the movie, *Deep Throat*. He should've known."

"And so you wanted your father to come looking for you, just like George C. Scott did in *Hard Core*?"

"Yeah. Sure. He should've done something. Anything."

twenty

I feel now that if my father had known what was happening to me, he would have rescued me. But he didn't know. And he didn't rescue me. Then I was off again, swept away by another storm of tears, while Laurendi waited patiently for me to calm down. What happened was that this whole line of thought had touched an even deeper sadness. It made me realize that I had passed my whole life without really coming to know my father.

How could the parent *not* know that his child was in trouble? Right now I feel so close to my own children, to Dominic and Lindsay, that if anything is ever hurting them, I'm sure I'll know about it. And do something about it. Even now I wonder why my parents couldn't see the hurt in my eyes. Why couldn't they see my pain and recognize that I was in trouble?

Why didn't they realize what was happening to their daughter?

The Flashback—

Late one afternoon, Chuck lying on the bed, cleaning his gun. A knock at the front door. My parents. A surprise visit. Chuck whispering to me, "Don't let them in yet. Before you open the door, take off your robe." Me pleading, "Chuck, those are my parents out there." Pointing the gun at my head: "Take that robe off right now or I'll fucking rip it off you. And if you let them know that this was my idea, I'm going to shoot you all. I mean that, babe. All three of you will be fucking dead on the floor."

Naked, walking to the door, opening it. My father blushing and looking away, my mother's mouth starting to tremble. Chuck throwing me a robe, saying, "Here, put on something decent. How could you answer a door like that? You should have clothes on in front of your own father."

They should have realized that "Linda Lovelace" wasn't their daughter. All of my life they had known me as a prude. They knew I wasn't sexy and I wasn't sexually driven. Maybe if I had gone in for that kind of thing before, or if I had shown even some hints of that kind of personality, then I could accept their hands-off attitude. But I had always been a goody-goody, and they knew that.

And that day, as I was taking the lie detector test, I found myself wondering whether anything had really changed, whether anything was better now. I loved my father a great deal, but we weren't talking at all; I never knew how to reach him.

My father tries to show his feelings, but it's never through talk. Still, I know he loves me. When he came to visit me not long ago the first thing he did was build a shelf in the baby's room. Then he helped me measure all the windows for plexiglas storm windows. And he fixed different things around the house that I didn't know how to repair. Then he hung up a planter for me. But, as usual, we didn't talk much. We have never talked much.

During that visit, my father and Larry started to talk. My father said that he had no idea I was ever in danger. He saw me playing out Chuck's script and he believed it to be the truth. "If I had known Chuck was hurting Linda," he told Larry, "I would have taken care of him then and there. I just didn't know."

My parents have come to visit me in my new home several times and everytime they leave, I cry. I cry so much. I'm always afraid this is going to be our last meeting. And there's so much that hasn't been said, so many things we haven't been able to say to each other.

"Are you ready to go on with the test?" Laurendi asked.

"I guess so."

After my breakdown, there were a few more questions and then Laurendi was through with me. As I left his office on the second day of testing, I didn't bother to ask him how I did. That was because I never doubted the outcome. I knew what the truth was and I trusted Nat Laurendi and his machine. I'd like to tell you that all of the others waiting for the verdict were equally confident— but I'm afraid that wasn't the case.

A few days later, my co-author returned to Laurendi's office to pick up the formal report. Unable to wait, he asked Laurendi what his honest opinion was.

"She's telling the truth." The polygraphist illustrated with the rolled-up charts. He showed my intentionally false answers to the sample questions, causing the needles to jump dramatically all over the page.

"This part of the test is very important," Laurendi said, "Because it shows that her past didn't interfere with the test. She is not emotionally bankrupt; she doesn't piss ice water; she is still a human being, regardless of all the things that happened to her in the past."

"Is there any chance that she could be fooling the machine?"

"Could she be conning me? No. She'd have to be some actress—and even if she were that good an actress, she couldn't control her blood pressure. These are true answers, they don't indicate any deception. Oh, here and there you'll see emotional responses as she relives her past—but those emotional responses come as I'm asking the question, not as she's answering. Basically, she's just not that good an actress. She's no Stanislavsky; she can't control her motivations. Have I seen actresses? Yes. Have I seen conmen? Yes. Is Linda one of these? No."

"So the test shows . . ."

"There are no reactions to indicate deception," he said. "There is absolutely no indication of deception."

And that's what the six-page, single-space typewritten report said, over and over again.

The report's bottom lines—

"Based upon the information supplied, the galleys of Ordeal, *the pre-polygraph test interviews prior to each phase of the test, the analysis of the emotional reactions on the polygraph to the above critical questions and post-test conversation and interrogation of Subject, it* is *my professional opinion that Subject's answers to the above critical questions were truthful."*

twenty-one

Lyle Stuart wanted my first book-promotion appearance to be on a nationally televised program. He selected Tom Snyder's *Tomorrow Show,* for our first stop. Another appearance would be on *Donahue.* Phil Donahue's program is always important to anyone who has a book to sell.

Snyder would be tough. I had seen him enough times to know that he could be brutal when he didn't believe someone. But if that show didn't go well, I'd always have *The Donahue Show* and Donahue was such a pussycat—that would be a cinch.

Wrong.

And wrong again.

At any rate, Tom Snyder was the first hurdle. That evening, in the studio waiting for the show to begin—by coincidence, it happened to be my 31st birthday—there was a great deal of nervousness. A great deal of nervousness, but it wasn't mine. My publisher, Lyle Stuart, was there with his top executives; so was my husband; so was my co-author; so were several lawyers who had become attached to the project. And some of them seemed very worried whether I'd be able to stand up to Tom Snyder.

Maybe I seemed a little edgy, but no one there could dream of how positive I felt. More than positive—elated. I had been waiting so long for the chance to step in front of the camera and tell my story simply and directly. This was it, my first national program, my first opportunity to tell millions of people—*millions* of people!—just what had happened and who was to blame and who was not to blame.

I knew that Tom Snyder on television could have an acid personality. Before we began, he gave me no clue as to what he thought of me or my book. It did help to see all those familiar faces there, even if they were a bit strained. For the first time in many years, it was no longer just Larry and me against the world. There were others now who were standing beside us.

Just before we went on camera, Tom Snyder exchanged a few words with me. He said a few things about one of the characters in the book, Al Goldstein, publisher of *Screw*, and he said that he thought Goldstein had become a good family man; he was always playing with his son and buying him presents. He said he was surprised to read of Goldstein's role in my life.

That was all he said—but it was enough to send a wave of fear through me. The moment the red light went on and we were on camera, however, I began to relax. Snyder was not at all antagonistic. He had gone to the trouble of reading the entire book; he had been shocked by it; and now he was matter-of-factly, but gently, guiding me through a retelling of the story. I'd been told that most television hosts don't have guts. But Tom Snyder had absolutely no hesitation about using the names of the famous and infamous who appeared in my book.

At one point Snyder asked me whether I felt the people connected with *Deep Throat* should be behind bars, and I said yes. I was definitely emotional and maybe overreacting; but it was a pleasure, after all those years, to finally take the offensive.

Snyder mentioned a name, and it was later to prompt the threat of a lawsuit unless there was a retraction. There was no retraction and no lawsuit.

I found myself really liking Tom Snyder. By the end of the hour I felt as though I was sitting there chatting with an old friend. He signed off by observing that I was obviously quite pregnant and he wished us "both" well.

Suddenly the waiting room was filled with smiles. No one had to say a word; I could tell from their faces that it had gone very well.

The show was taped several hours ahead of its actual air-time so Larry and I raced to get home in time to see it. But I'd been away from the limelight too long. Too many years of early-to-bed-and-early-to-rise. And perhaps the excitement of the day had been too much for me. All I know is that by the time my premiere performance began—my long-awaited debut on national television—both Larry and I had fallen asleep.

I managed to stir myself toward the end of the show, waking for a minute or two, just long enough to see whether I looked all right, but this was one night I went to sleep without a care in the world.

After that there were many television interviews, and some of them were excellent. One of the best was a young man named Gene Taylor in Detroit. Before I came onto his show, he had gone to the trouble of making still photographs from *Deep Throat*, photographs that showed the bruises all over my body. Before we began talking, he showed those photos on camera. After the show, on learning that Larry and I had run out of money, he reached into his pocket and lent us a hundred dollars.

Another memorable show was a Chicago interview conducted by a psychiatrist. It turned out that he had specialized in treating boys and girls who were youthful victims of pornography. As the program came to an end, he told me there was only one major difference between my story and hundreds of other stories he knew about—my story had a happy ending; I was alive and free.

He told me that many of the women who were trapped

in the pornography underworld wound up in alleyways with their arms marked by needles; the police would then assume they were prostitutes who had overdosed when, in reality, they might be young girls who had been used by pornographers and pimps and then junked.

And, of course, there were low spots as well. I remember one radio show where the host seemed both understanding and sympathetic. Then, during the commercial break, his attitude changed completely; he tried to make it sound as though we were accomplices playing a little joke on the public. He turned to me and said, "Do you know what my favorite line in *Deep Throat* is? It's really become a classic. That's where the girl says, 'Do you mind if I smoke while you're eating?'"

Larry looked up at that. I knew my husband well enough to realize that another interview had just come to an early end. The commercial was still playing as Larry got to his feet.

"Linda, are you about done here?" he said. "We've heard about enough of this bullshit."

"This show's not over," the interviewer said.

"You think not?" Larry said. "Come on, Linda. If this guy's got any more questions, he can answer them himself."

The lowest spot of all was a television interview conducted in New York by Stanley Siegel.

Before that show began, the producer took me aside and asked me what I wanted to talk about and what I didn't want to talk about. I told her the things that bothered me the most. And then I began to relax under the misapprehension that this would be a gentle and polite interview.

"What does it feel like to have sex with five men at the same time?" I was asked.

I may not have the exact wording and I can no longer remember my answer. But I went into an immediate state of shock; it seemed almost as bad as the days when I was

being beaten. I looked over at Larry; his face was frozen.
Later, when we talked it over, we discovered we had both
felt the same emotions. My instinct was to get up and walk
off the stage without another word. But at the same time I
was plagued by doubts: Was that allowed? What would
happen to the show? Would I be letting down my publisher and my co-author?

The questions go no better. Stanley Siegel went after
sensation for sensation's sake. I kept thinking that I had to
get out of there, away from him, but I didn't know what to
do, or what to say. Today, it would be different. Today I
would get up, spit in his face and storm away.

Finally, after he dredged up all the muck he could think
of, the interview came to an end. As the show's final commercial was being played, he turned to Larry and said,
"How do you think it went?"

"It sucks," Larry said, using a word he understandably
reserved for only the worst offenses. It was not difficult for
Siegel to see how upset I was. But then, you didn't have to
be terribly perceptive to observe that I was weeping.

"I'm sorry," he said.

"If you're really sorry," Larry said, "let's do it over."

"Oh, I couldn't do that," he said.

As Siegel walked away, the producer who had asked the
pre-show questions, apologized for his performance: "I
can't understand it, he wasn't supposed to ask any of those
things."

As we drove home from Manhattan that day, we realized
that we were on unfamiliar turf. We knew so little about
the world of television and television interviewers, what
was allowed or not allowed.

However, if anyone came to our home and spoke to me
the way Stanley Siegel had just done, he would be carried
out. I didn't know then that the producer was as disturbed
as I was. She called Lyle Stuart and said, "Immediately
after the show, I told him, 'Stanley, you're a pig. We can't
use this tape. You look and sound like a dirty old man.' "

There were other bad interviewers—some of them cynical and hostile—but none bothered me so much as Siegel. Most of the time I could see a negative attitude as a challenge. Maybe I would be able to open their eyes to other possibilities.

As the interviews continued and I was exposed to every possible question, the main problem became one of repetition. How do you avoid sounding like a broken record when you're always giving the same answers to the same questions?

And the questions were always the same. "How come you couldn't get away?" and "Why didn't you call the police?" and "How is Chuck Traynor doing now?" and "If you were telling the truth, how come he's not is jail?" A funny thing had happened. Although this had been a story I was dying to tell, the repetition was killing the good feelings. Flying from one city to the next, speaking to faces that blurred together into a composite interviewer, I began to hate the sound of my voice telling the same story at every whistlestop.

The interview of greatest importance was *The Donahue Show*. I felt pressure—but no real fear. If tough Tom Snyder was gentle, there was certainly no reason to be alarmed by Phil Donahue—he was gentle to start with. However, as soon as we went on the air, I sensed that something was not . . . quite . . . right. Donahue was reserved and cool, maybe even a bit standoffish.

"Let's begin by taking a survey," he greeted his audience. "First, how many here know who Linda Lovelace is? You have to . . ."

Applause interrupted him.

"How many think it's all right for her to write her book and tell her story and . . .?"

More applause.

"You really think it's all right?" he said. "How many think it's an effort just to make money?"

Applause.

Donahue was leading the audience the way a conductor leads an orchestra. Anyone who watches the *The Donahue Show* knows the audience follows his leads very closely. It's no secret that his audience—and, in fact, most women in America—love Phil Donahue. And whenever he begins a new line of thought, his audience picks up on it quickly.

And then he turned to me.

"You know, thinking of you with a bungalow and a vegetable garden and a white picket is just a killer; you know what I mean."

"I love it," I said. "I really do."

"I know. But, my dear, you've lived on two different planets now."

"Yeah, well, actually, that wasn't me back then," I said. "This is me now. I finally can be myself, you know, and I have everything I've wanted."

"Sure. How did you get involved with all that stuff? I mean, how could a nice girl like you—how do you answer that?"

I answered it the way I had answered it in the book. The way a nice girl like me gets caught up in Linda Lovelace's life is through sheer brute force. I went over that again—how I'd been beaten and imprisoned and threatened; how I'd been forced to live out the most extreme sexual fantasies that a sick mind could invent; how I had lived more than two years in the close company of death, worried about both my life and the lives of my parents.

Donahue seemed to wonder whether all this was a voluntary act on my part, whether I had *willingly* given up my freedom.

"Apparently," Donahue observed, "there are a lot of young women who are similarly trapped by Jim Jones kinds of people. I'm not for a minute attempting to equate anybody with that personality in Guyana, but the circumstances of being emotionally attached to a person, even one who knocks you around, is apparently—it exists in a number of places in this country . . . Is there anything about the way you were raised, in your view, that made you vulnerable to this?"

"Well, I was very naïve," I said. "I knew nothing about sex. I had no—you know, my mother and father never talked to me about it. I think if I had known a little more, possibly—but that's hard. I don't think there's any real way to warn somebody about a Chuck Traynor."

"But you did not feel close to your parents, did you?"

"No, there wasn't that total closeness. We were very close until I was about 16, and then we started to drift apart. My father and I were always very close, but that had to end."

"Yeah, but I mean—all right, this is very amateur analysis, but see . . . one of the things, one of the really valuable things about talking to you is it might help us figure out how to make sure our kids don't get . . ."

He kept going deeper and deeper into the way I'd been raised. The difficulty in communicating with my parents. Their strictness. Someone had to be blamed for what had happened to me and apparently he had decided to fix blame on my parents. It seemed to me that the blame belonged to my captor, Chuck Traynor, and to all the men who bought me and rented me and used me and abused me.

Later on members of the audience were invited to stand up to say their pieces. One woman pointed out that she had gone through hard times as a child but she had enough moral fiber so that it was never necessary for her to become a . . . Linda Lovelace.

"A lot of us had this going on when we were teenagers, and we didn't go the route you went," she said. "How do you account for this? You talk about being a protected child and staying home and your mother wanted to know where you were . . . I didn't just go off the deep end and say, well, you know, she wants to know where I am, therefore I'm going to be as promiscuous as I want to be, I'll fix her."

"What do you mean by 'promiscuous'?" I asked. "You lost me there."

"Being naughty and bad," Donahue explained.

"Oh, but that was not by choice," I had to explain all over again. "I didn't do that as a resentment towards my parents."

It took time, nearly the full hour, but finally I felt I was winning the audience over. By the end of the show Donahue himself had become softer and more understanding. Still, the discussion took many directions I didn't like—the importance of parents and upbringing and childhood in all the awful things that had happened to me.

Finally, at the very end of the program, I tried to get in a brief defense of my mother.

"I want to say something here," I blurted out. "I don't hate my mother at all. I think there's a very good chance that my mother was also a victim of Mr. Traynor's because if you were looking at a white piece of paper he could convince you that it was black. And I think . . . I don't hate my mother for not understanding."

Putting the blame on my parents is too easy; it lets everyone else off the hook. True, many battered housewives began life as battered children. There's surely something to the notion that childhood beatings condition people to respond to beatings received later in life. And so some people might conclude that since my mother hit me from time to time, that's the reason I became one of history's more famous battered women.

This theme was later picked up by the press. Some printed reports came down as hard on my mother as on Chuck Traynor. For a time this all but destroyed my relations with my parents. To read some of the stories, you'd think my mother was another Mommie Dearest—but, to me, she was but a tiny part of my strife.

Of course it's not Donahue's business to be either on my side or against me. But I did feel he was standing up high on some moral ground, looking down at me from a height I'd obviously never attain.

"Linda, you really were and are—but especially in the early seventies—you were quite a celebrity. Everybody talked about you. There's always a giggle and a joke that goes with the mention . . . all conversations about you include a normal statement that comes out dirty because of the context. Do you know what I mean?"

"Yes."

"That's an awful way for you—that's going to follow you forever."

Oh, God, I hoped not! Why on earth had I written the book then?

"No, I don't think so," I insisted. "I really don't. I think once people realize who I really am, and that Linda Lovelace was a fictitious creation of Chuck Traynor's, and a robot that just functioned to survive, and they get to know me and how I really am, I think a lot of it might stop. I hope so."

"You learned a lot," he said. "Yeah. You learned about hooking, too, didn't you? I mean, at least you were obliged to be a prostitute?"

Maybe I was listening between the lines but what I was hearing was disapproval.

"You embarrassed some very important people in this book."

"Well, I don't know how you mean 'important people.' "

"Well, okay, let me say *famous* people."

"Well, famous people—but, you know, they're all, in my opinion, in one way or another, just as bad as Chuck Traynor was. And they participated for their own satisfaction and didn't do anything to try to help me."

"But did they *know*?" he asked. "I mean, is it *fair*?"

"It sound like I picked them out because they're important people. No. They were just a part of the ordeal that I went through."

"Is it fair to have expected them to understand entirely the slave kind of thing you were under? I mean, they would only see you on weekends of whenever. Here's the thing: I'm not forgiving anybody but, you know, if a guy has a couple of beers and you come in looking like you did then, I'm not forgiving it—it's just that . . . is putting him in a book that's going to sell a whole lot of copies necessarily a redeeming thing to do?"

It was never my intention to hurt an innocent bystander. I didn't create their lifestyles; their lifestyles existed long before I came along and long after I left.

"Well," I said, "I felt it was important to let everything out that happened to me. And to leave someone out because they're important or they have a name, I didn't think that was right, you know."

"But you know, " Donahue broke in, "they have families, too, and you know, and kids—do you think about this?"

"No."

It was difficult, even in my wildest imaginings, to think of Hugh Hefner as a family man. Some of the others I mentioned in the book—the closest they ever came to a family was the Colombo family.

Finally, the show was over and Phil Donahue was walking away. Larry, standing in the wings, called out to the famous television host.

"Hey, *you*!"

"What?" Donahue asked.

"I want to talk to you."

"What's the matter?"

"Why'd you do that?" Larry wasn't lowering his voice. "Why'd you defend those people and hurt my wife?"

"That's not my business," Donahue said, "That's between them and their psychiatrists."

Then he walked away. And the show—the most important show I would do— was over. And while I will always feel badly about some parts of it, I know that viewers saw it as an interesting hour of give and take. Oh, maybe I took more than I gave—but this was what I had been waiting for, the opportunity to tell my story to the widest possible audience.

If I could judge by the studio audience, I seemed to have some impact. One of the women there stood up and said that she had been bothered when she came into the auditorium that morning and learned that the guest for the day was . . . Linda Lovelace.

"But I'm really enjoying this," she said. "I have to admit that I'm afraid when I heard who was going to be the guest, I thought, 'Oh, dear!' You're just a lovely lady, and thank you for being here."

"I don't blame you," I said. "I feel the same way. I would never want to meet Linda Lovelace either."

There was one other question that didn't mean as much to me at that moment but would mean a great deal to me as time went on. A woman stood up and said, "Other women are involved in probably doing things against their will—isn't this a feminist question? What are they . . . what is the feminist movement, or any feminist organization—are *they* involved in helping these women?"

"I really don't know too much about that."

That was understating the case.

But I was to learn.

Because *The Phil Donahue Show*—good in parts, bad in parts—was by far the most important thing to happen to me or to my book. Wherever that show played in the weeks that followed, *Ordeal* was sure to sell out. And by the time the show had run its course around the country, the book was on every best-seller list in America.

And there were two other results of that telecast that was of even greater importance to me.

One: Gloria Steinem happened to be watching.

Two: And so was a woman named Patricia. That's the name she signed to a postcard she sent me that I still keep in my bedroom under a statue of the Blessed Mother: "Dear Linda. Thank you. I got out. Your interview with Donahue was wonderful for me. Again, thank you."

twenty-two

People may think being on a publicity tour is a glamorous experience but that's not the way it works out. I was pregnant and tired and hounded by old demons that the questions kept reawakening. Sometimes I reacted badly. As when I would land in a strange town and find that the hotel didn't have a reservation for me. Or come into an airport and have to wait two or three hours for a car to arrive. Or be unable to eat at a restaurant because my picture was in all the local newspapers.

After weeks on tour, I began to feel the pressure. Larry, on the other hand, was settling down. It may have been the fact that I was being taken seriously by most of the interviewers; or it may have been the lithium. Whatever the reason, it was a welcome change. The irony was that as Larry returned to his old self, I became unglued.

The climax came one night near the end of the tour. It was 4 a.m. and I was in Manhattan, alone on a deserted city street. I stopped at a public telephone and dialed Mike McGrady's home number. He awakened from a deep sleep and heard a voice right out of *The Exorcist*.

"Mike? Mike! I'm so frightened! He's coming after me! He's looking for me everywhere!"

"Who *is* this?"

"It's Linda—I need help, oh, God, I need help!"

"Linda, calm down," he said, coming fully awake. "Just calm down. Calm down and tell me what's going on."

"Chuck is chasing me," I said. "Chuck is trying to kill me."

"*Chuck?* Where is he now?"

"He's just up the street. He's been after me for hours. He's calling for me. He's looking everywhere. I'm hiding in this phone booth. I'm so frightened."

"Linda, where's Larry? Did you call the cops?"

"Mike, you've got to help me—what can I do?"

"Linda, I'm a hundred miles away. Tell me where you are. What street are you on? Listen now. You have to get out of there. You're got to get a policeman—*did* you call the cops?"

"They said they're on their way. Oh, I can see him— Chuck's just up the block. He's looking for me."

"Linda, tell me where you are—what's the address there?—I'll call the cops, too."

"Oh, God, Mike, he's *here!* I—"

And that's all my co-author heard, the end of a call that would keep him awake the rest of the night. I turned to face my attacker. Chuck was now almost upon me.

"Get away from me," I snarled at him. "Don't you dare touch me!"

"What're you talking about?" he said. "C'mon honey, take it easy now."

"Leave me alone, Chuck. The cops will be here any second."

"I'm *not* Chuck," he said. "It's me. It's Larry. Come on, Linda, I've been looking for you everywhere. We've got to go back to the hotel room now. We both need a good night's sleep."

Blame it on the pressures of the tour. I don't know exactly what happened and I don't know why it happened. But for four hours I became convinced that Larry was Chuck, and that my life was again in danger.

There were too many pressures on me. When people question your honesty every day of your life, you begin to wonder what is and what isn't real. If anyone had seen me on this craziest of nights, I would have lost all credibility.

The next morning, back in the hotel room, I woke up alone. Larry was sleeping on the couch on the other side of the room. I had a small hangover and some vague memories of running down city streets in my bare feet.

"Larry," I called over to him, "why are you sleeping on the couch?"

"Huh?" he said. "You don't remember?"

"Remember what?"

All I could remember was tripping on the sidewalk about midnight. Larry filled in some of the spaces. After falling, I started calling my husband "Chuck" and running from him. I spent the pre-dawn hours playing hide-and-seek through the streets of Manhattan. I was shocked to learn that I'd telephoned the police and my co-author.

Okay, it was just one incident. I could accept that. I decided not to let it bother me so much. And it didn't. I went on with the tour and then—*pow!*—it happened again. Twice. Different circumstances, different people, different surroundings—but again I was calling my husband "Chuck" and running from him.

A touch of paranoia? Perhaps. It was as if I had traded places with Larry. There are still times when I don't trust anyone at all, times when I feel that everyone is out to get me. Maybe that's understandable. But what seems to trigger it is alcohol; on each occasion when there's been an incident, there was quite a bit of wine to drink beforehand. That's another reason I no longer drink.

The oddest thing is that I was no longer so afraid of Chuck. My feeling about Chuck is that he probably didn't mind *Ordeal* at all; he'd see that as some kind of advertisement.

As I went around the country telling my story to both television and print reporters, the stress mounted. Linda Lovelace had always been fair game and an easy target. And since the press had long ago made up its mind about me, I had my work cut out for me.

It could not have seemed simpler. I just had to explain to the press flat-out that there were *two* Lindas; one was a lie, one was the truth.

The lie, needless to say, was the Linda Lovelace who appeared in *Deep Throat* and books like *Inside Linda*

Lovelace. The lie was the girl with a clitoris in her throat. The lie was the insatiable 21-year-old girl who only lived to give pleasure to men, whose sole pleasure, in fact, was the amount of pleasure she was able to provide. But why on earth would anyone have to point out that this was a lie? What kind of person could possible see this fantasy as truth in the first place?

The truth, unfortunately, was not nearly so exciting. More logical, more ordinary, more sane—but not so exciting. The truth was: Linda Marchiano, a 31-year-old woman, married, pregnant with her second child, spending all of her energy scraping by, trying to keep her family together, trying to make ends meet. The truth was: a woman who wanted only the simplest things—a family who loves her and is loved by her, a small home, a garden.

Who could ever imagine that the press would scoff at aspirations this modest?

Now that the experience is over, there are two things I don't understand, two things I'll never understand.

One is the way the press swallowed such a self-evident lie.

Two is the great difficulty it had accepting an equally obvious truth.

And now I'm talking about *all* segments of the press—the book publishers who gave us such a hard time, the television giants, the newspaper reporters, the magazine interviewers, everyone right down to, and including, the phone-in disk jockeys from Tucson and Albuquerque.

At the beginning of my post-*Ordeal* ordeal, I had two pieces of evidence. First, myself. I was willing to go anywhere and answer any questions. I've learned that people who have a chance to see me as I'm telling my story are generally won over. (Not all of them, to be sure, but most of them.) Secondly, I had the book. The book was as ugly, as horrifying, as sordid as the experience itself had been. Nothing—none of the grotesque details, none of the famous names—had been changed. It was all there, all hanging out. I didn't think anyone could read that whole book and still feel I was telling a lie.

twenty-three

Before the tour, the world knew nothing about the book. The first public mention of it was a standard description in Lyle Stuart's catalogue. The first media mention came in the New York *Post*: "Linda (*Deep Throat*) Lovelace, perhaps the most famous (and uniquely talented) porn star ever, clearly reveled in the glory of it all when her first film came out in the early '70s. Now she has emerged from recent obscurity to tell a different story. Not totally emerged, of course; actually, she says she has gone into hiding to escape years of unspeakable sexual tortures—and the celebrities who made her undergo them. Naturally, said celebs will be named in the little book titled *Ordeal* Ms. Lovelace happens to be putting on paper with the help of a writer."

"*Most uniquely talented.*" What does that tell us about the mindset of the man—for man it had to be—who wrote that? I soon learned there are many ways of calling a person a liar without ever actually using the word "liar."

The first mentions of the book were all loaded with innuendo, with sarcasm, with the same attitudes that confronted the old Linda Lovelace. There were times when you didn't exactly have to be an expert at reading between the lines. The London *Daily Mail* asked, "But why has Ms. Lovelace waited so long to unburden her soul? Why is she now talking with such remarkable earnestness? The answer is simple: Ms. Lovelace has a book to sell."

As these first reactions arrived, I became increasingly depressed. One day I called my co-author: "I *knew* it wouldn't work! It was stupid to think we could change the mind of the world! The whole book is a waste of time!"

"It's too early to tell," he said. "Those people making the comments haven't had a chance to read the book yet. All they're doing is shooting from the hip."

"Yeah, but why do I always have to be the target?"

"Patience," he said. "It's going to take time but it's going to happen."

Larry had a different attitude: "They'll never believe it," he said. "It's hopeless to try and convince them."

Things didn't get much better when the magazines came out. *Playboy*, ran an old picture of me (naked, naturally) with the words, "And Linda Lovelace hops onto the bandwagon with *Ordeal*, in which she claims she was forced into *Deep Throat*."

Al Goldstein also ran an announcement, complete with nude photos, in *Screw*, his publication for perverts. Goldstein, too, had been an active participant in my most degraded moments. Those *Screw* subscribers able to read would have seen this story:

"It sounds to us like nothing more than another cheap attempt to cash in on the thriving memoir market. As we remember it, Linda didn't look one bit dissatisfied in that loop she did with a dog . . . We don't doubt Linda got fucked over. She was part of an era in which most X-rated performers were routinely exploited. But what a shoddy way to attempt a comeback!"

I was surprised to find that one nugget of truth (" . . . X-rated performers were routinely exploited") gleaming through the muck. This is what I've been saying all along, of course, and generally to angry denials by those who have done—and continue to do—most of the exploiting. I'm pleased to note that this most authoritative of pornographic sources agrees with me.

I was terribly depressed. It took weeks for me to rationalize it. What did I want, praise from *Screw*? However, all these early reactions showed me what we were up against.

And I'll admit to real doubt, to wondering whether anyone would ever believe me.

The first reviews didn't give me much cause for hope. Some of the reviewers tended to ignore the book and decided to review me as a human being. Someone named Larry Wilson wrote, "I was always at a loss to understand the appeal of either Lovelace or *Deep Throat*. She was rather unattractive, not even the usual soft-focus airbrush photography of *Playboy* could make her appealing."

There was an incredibly disturbing unsigned review in the Boston *Globe*: "Educational as this collaboration may be, it hardly inspires you to reach for your handkerchief. As has been said recently about a different subject altogether, what we need nowadays is a better class of victim."

Just when I was beginning to think that what I needed was a better class of reviewer, we began to get some friendlier notices. Interestingly enough, all the friendly notices came from women.

To see the male-female split on reactions to my book, one only has to contrast the favorable reviews written by women with the review printed in *Playboy*. That magazine attacked my book a second time without ever bothering to mention that *Playboy* publisher Hugh Hefner was a central figure: "What's interesting is *Ordeal* is just as lurid and graphic as any of her films. In fact, for a reformed woman, she seems to dwell inordinately on the seamier side of her life, making sure to mention all the famous people she claims to have had affairs with . . ."

I never expected the press to automatically believe something just because it was written down on a piece of paper. But I had no idea there would be such automatic disbelief among men.

Reporters would express great sympathy, would tell me they believed me all the way, and then would put things in the article saying just the opposite. Later they'd explain that their stories had been heavily edited. But I had to wonder whether they were afraid of looking gullible in front of their bosses.

It was a familiar pattern. The reporter would come in and say, "I believe your book and I'm glad you lived to tell the tale," or words to that effect. Then the article would be filled with "she claimed" and "she insisted" and "on the other hand."

I noticed a big difference between the way the press treated me this time and during the days I was Linda Lovelace, supersexstar. Back then the reporter would come in almost glowing, supercharged with interest, not knowing what to expect. (Of course, back then neither the reporter nor I knew what Chuck Traynor was going to order me to do for the journalist's entertainment.)

This time the interviews were somber and the reporters tended to be subdued. My general impression: Reporters had been more interested in meeting Linda Lovelace, super-freak, than they were in meeting Linda Marchiano, suburbanite housewife and mother.

Naturally, I'm human enough to like those reporters who came over to my side. When I first met Marian Christy of the Boston *Globe* I thought she was going to do a hatchet job. But she listened closely. And she didn't just listen with her ears, she listened with her heart. Lynn Darling of the Washington *Post* did a fair and balanced report. Karen Payne of *People* magazine was sympathetic.

Typical of the men covering the story was Chip Visci of the Detroit *Free Press*: "Lie detector tests notwithstanding, believing her story at all, much less immediately, is not easy. Many who have seen *Deep Throat* or another, even sleazier film in which her co-star was a dog, will argue that Linda Lovelace liked what she was doing, and liked it a lot."

Liked it a lot—can you believe that? Can you imagine what kind of person could feel that any woman would actually *like* having sex with a dog? Deep in his story, Visci revealed what was bothering him the most. Not really that my story was unbelievable; it's that it just wasn't sexy enough.

"Ultimately, Mrs. Marchiano's story is believable," he writes, "especially when you consider that many battered wives refuse to leave their husbands. Believable but not very readable. The language is crude and profane, the sexual descriptions not at all erotic. The book has a hard-edged matter-of-fact-tone."

The book, then, just wasn't erotic enough. Would some people read the diary of an Auschwitz survivor and wonder why it wasn't sexier, more amusing?

Visci's attitude upset me; I was even more disturbed by the writers who did, in fact, find the book erotic. Especially when the reporter came from my home-town newspaper, *Newsday*. This feature writer found a book that was ". . . steamy, brutal, sexually graphic . . . a sex-drenched record . . . So there it is, the Linda Lovelace story at $10 a throw. It is, to put it one way, titillating."

Titillating? When I looked that up in my dictionary, I found "to excite a tingling sensation" or "to excite agreeably." All in all I'd say that *Ordeal* was about as titillating as Hiroshima. But maybe you had to be there.

Women, on the other hand, tended to take me seriously. A Canadian writer, Judith Finlayson, seemed to side with me: "As I understand it, Lovelace was successful as a porn queen because she had the fresh scrubbed good looks of the girl next door, and enough dramatic ability to convince the camera that she loves being degraded. What does that say about the mainstream men who flocked in droves to see the film?"

Another writer, Joy Fielding, asked a logical question: Why had the protests from all the men named in my book been so mild as to be inaudible? "Perhaps it is because they felt that ultimately no one would believe this gruesome memoir, that she would be dismissed as a woman only out to make a buck, out to out-confess Britt and Joan and all the others who slept with Warren and Ryan, that she would be laughed at as a woman clutching at the straws of fame that had long since deserted her . . . People may open this book with a snicker; they will not be laughing when they close it."

There was no way to mistake the phenomenon: Women tended to believe me and most men thought I was lying.

Why this split? What was at the root of it?

Maybe women didn't find my story all that far-fetched. Surely I was an extreme case—maybe even *the* extreme case—but many women have experienced at least some moments of terror at the hands of a man. From time to time women do encounter sadists and other creeps. Perhaps they never went through the suffering I did but they knew it was at least possible. Surely there were some who felt: There, but for the grace of God, go I. My story was gruesome, but women knew it was possible.

What about the male attitude?

I began to feel maybe it was connected to the phenomenal success of *Deep Throat*. After all, why *was* this one movie so successful? Some hit movies play in the same theater for ten weeks; *Deep Throat* played in some theaters for ten *years*! The box office receipts from one theater alone, the one in San Francisco, have come to more than $6.5 million. The total take? Experts have estimated the gross at more than $300 million, which would make it more profitable than *Star Wars*.

Some explain this success by saying *Deep Throat* was the first porn movie with a sense of humor. If there was any humor there, it never quite reached locker-room level. The photography was nothing special. None of the actors have gone on to win Academy Awards or even to become better known for their work in other films.

Others give me full credit for the film's success. Thanks, but no thanks. They say it was because I was not the usual bleached blonde with pumped-up breasts but a young fresh-looking girl who always managed a pretty smile no matter what revolting things were done to her.

I happen to think the reason for the movie's success was the story line. I don't know whether writer-director Gerard

Damiano understood the power of the male fantasy he chose, or whether it was just one of those unhappy accidents. What was that story line?

A woman with a clitoris in her throat!

That's the whole story of *Deep Throat*. A woman with a clitoris in her throat. A woman who receives immense, bell-ringing gratification only through the act of oral sex.

Damiano composed the entire story line, not to mention the title tune, during a single drive from Brooklyn to Manhattan. But did he ever suspect that his shoddy little $22,000 movie would strike such a responsive chord? Could he have guessed that this notion of a woman getting pleasure only through oral sex would prove so exciting to so many men? Who would have guessed that this one sordid freak show would lead to million-dollar offers, book contracts, stage shows and the name Linda Lovelace becoming as well known as any name in the land?

And all this because I was a figment of the male imagination, a creature from some perverse male fantasy. The basic oral sex fantasy—sex without effort, sex without involvement, sex without hassle, sex without any effort on the man's part.

I think that's why men came by the million to see *Deep Throat*, to see Linda Lovelace smiling her idiot smile no matter what was being forced down her gullet. Men must've looked at that and thought: well, it *looks* like she's having a great time so she must *be* having a great time. They wanted to believe the fantasy so badly that no one seemed to notice the huge black-and-blue marks on my body.

Sure, oral sex can be part of making love. But I believe men who want it to be the whole thing, the *only* thing, are warped. And no wonder so many women came away from that movie feeling upset. Men who get a charge from that movie are buying the notion that women are meant to be used. They don't see women as equal partners in sex or anything else.

At this point, I still didn't know what was going to happen to my book. Did anyone really believe the story? Was I getting through to anyone? Or was I doomed to be always what I had been ten years earlier: A bad joke—the Linda Lovelace doll; wind her up and she swallows the key.

twenty-four

Gloria Steinem happened to see me on *The Donahue Show*. What did I know about Gloria Steinem at that time? Even less than she knew about me. Which is to say, nothing.

All I knew about Gloria Steinem was that she was associated in some way with a magazine called *Ms.* or *Mrs.* and was a woman who wanted to open her own doors and light her own cigarettes but not go out Dutch treat.

Ten years earlier, when everyone else was discovering feminism, it barely dented my consciousness. At that time I was the personal property of a pimp. What would something like that have to do with me?

How did Chuck Traynor react to feminism? I can tell you exactly. Did you ever see any of those vampire movies? And do you remember the big scene where the vampire is suddenly shown a cross? That's the way Chuck reacted to feminism.

When I was with Chuck—that was the first time people started asking each other whether they'd rather be called "Miss" or "Ms." One time Chuck snarled at me, "You can forget that 'Ms.' stuff—no *real* woman would ever want to be called 'Ms.'" That, of course, settled the issue.

Back then that was the entire feminist struggle to me, the only feminist issue—whether to be called "Miss" or "Ms." To me, it was immaterial; all I was ever called was "Hey-you." And when Chuck decided the whole issue was "a crock," I could see no reason to argue with him. Not that I ever would.

Now I see feminism as the exact opposite of everything Chuck believed and practiced. Often he explained to me that a woman's body was meant to make money so that a man would never have to go to work. Therefore, a "real woman" would do anything and everything that a "real man" commanded.

But Chuck didn't know any more about feminism than I did. I don't believe he ever read a book in his life. No, I take that back. He did read one book several times. It was called *The Family* and it was about the Charles Manson family; Manson was Chuck's idol.

I had never met any woman who described herself as a feminist. No one ever tried to get me to join the National Organization of Women or to back the Equal Rights Amendment or to get involved in any of the causes that feminists get involved in. Of course, people in pornography have never been noted for feminist sentiments. And people struggling to survive on welfare don't have the time or the energy to think about such things.

A hooker I worked with named Melody tried to be my friend. She gave me a book called *The Female Eunuch* by Germaine Greer. It was about the way men had always treated women. But when Chuck saw what I was about to read, he snatched it from my hands and threw it into the garbage.

In retrospect, I'm a little surprised that I didn't run into more feminists in the days when I was Linda Lovelace. I'm surprised they weren't out picketing me. I had to be Public Enemy Number One—this female freak who got such immense pleasure from serving men with oral sex.

But I never heard a peep from any of them. No one ever told me there were groups who could help someone like myself escape, groups that worked with battered women. If I'd known about these groups, I might have turned to them.

I've since learned that most big cities have special units set up to help women who are being abused by men. Now when a woman writes me or calls me asking for help—say a woman who has read *Ordeal* and finds herself in a similar situation—I refer her to a local feminist group.

But at that time my ignorance on these matters was awesome. When I heard that Gloria Steinem was trying to reach me, it meant nothing at all. She contacted Mike McGrady to say that she had seen me on *The Donahue Show* and wanted to learn more about me.

Not that she was instantaneously persuaded of the truth of my story. She grilled Mike on many details. Then she spoke to publisher Lyle Stuart's wife, Carole, and asked whether she was "crazy" to be concerned about my case. Both Carole and Mike assured her the story was true, and that I needed and deserved all the support I could get.

Once she was convinced, Gloria managed to get a message to me: If I needed any help at all, I should call her. How many times has Gloria given that same message to a woman in distress? I couldn't guess. But since I've come to know her, I've learned delivering that message is part of her life. In point of fact, she once delivered that same message to Marilyn Chambers, Chuck Traynor's new porn property.

Gloria and I were scheduled to appear on the same television program in New York City, a talk show called *Midday Live* hosted by Bill Boggs. One newspaper described our joint appearance, accurately enough, under this headline: "Odd Couplings."

Gloria wanted to interview me for an article. I went to her office before going to the television studio. I had never seen *Ms* magazine before. Now I know the kind of woman who reads *Ms* is someone who is independent and stands up for what she believes, the kind of woman who makes up her own mind about things. I wouldn't have qualified for a subscription back then.

My first impressions of Gloria were all positive and nothing has ever happened to change them. Everyone knows that she's attractive, intelligent, strong and independent. However, I'm not sure everyone knows how kind she is and how much she extends herself for people who are less fortunate.

Quite a few women were waiting to say hello to me at the *Ms* offices. That morning I met several of the most famous writers in the feminist movement—Susan Brownmiller, Andrea Dworkin, Letty Cottin Progrebin and others. At first they were just friendly people who wanted to help. Since then, some have become friends.

But that first day I knew nothing about any of them. All I knew is they were sizing me up. Whenever I'm in a setting like that, or with people who are celebrated and cultured, I become nervous. I always feel insecure around people who have gone to college, and these were all well-educated women; they were knowledgable, they were independent and they seemed oh-so-sure of themselves. These were people who knew what had gone on in society in a way I never will; they were able to make sense of things.

And, of course, they were all deeply involved in a women's movement of which I knew nothing.

At first I was surprised at the lack of hostility. It was as if there had never been hostility. These women had every reason to despise Linda Lovelace for the Big Lie she represented, but they greeted me with warmth.

twenty-five

As we began speaking I learned that Linda Lovelace had been one of their biggest obstacles to overcome. They explained: Whenever they went out to speak against pornography, the name "Linda Lovelace" was always thrown up to them. They'd always hear some variation of this: "How can you say that pornography is degrading to women? Look at Linda Lovelace—she always smiled and enjoyed it." My book was taking ammunition away from their opponents.

I was with friends. And Larry felt the same way. My husband always stays by my side on tours and during interviews, he can be tight as a drum, always on the lookout. He sensed at once these women would never work against my interests.

As we learned what feminism was all about—basically it has to do with fair play—we both realized there was nothing wrong with being a feminist. Although Larry knew nothing about feminism—and, in fact, had the typical set of male reactions to the whole notion—he now tells everyone that he's a feminist and, what's more, he is.

I think the whole experience has helped our marriage. Larry has always had a great deal of trouble accepting my past life. In his head, he knows I was a victim, but in his heart, he has to wonder why all this happened to me. Was there something about me, some weakness that led to my downfall? The feminists made us aware of the fact that I was just a statistic, just one of many women who have been defeated by a system that stacks the odds against them. The fact that I was not the only one helped Larry a great deal.

If I were just to list the things Gloria has done for me, it would fill several pages of this book. I've met many people who've spoken nice words to me. But every now and then a person comes along who backs up words with deeds. That's Gloria Steinem.

That was clear from the moment we met. After the television show we stood together on a streetcorner waiting for the show's limousine. The car failed to appear and we were stranded—stranded and vulnerable. I don't suppose I'll ever be able to stand on a crowded street without feeling some fear. When it was clear that the car was not coming, Gloria did a very typical thing. She simply arranged for another limousine to take us to our home a hundred miles away, and she paid for it herself.

I think it's possible to be more than a friend without ever quite being a buddy or a pal. I mean, when I'm depressed, blue, down in the dumps, I can't just call Gloria in the hope that she'll cheer me up. She's way too busy for that kind of thing.

But it's funny the kind of effect just knowing someone like Gloria can have on your life. Just knowing there are women who are strong and independent, women who are winners. My little daughter Lindsay is extremely independent, but if I see her not following her own mind or allowing some little boy to push her around, I'll hear myself saying, "Come on, Lindsay, I don't think Gloria would like that."

Some people ask me whether the woman's movement is using me a bit. It's only natural they would use me as an example of what can happen to a woman involved in pornography. This is the way I *want* to be used, these are the causes I *want* to be involved in. My relationship with feminism has never been one-sided. They use me to show people what can happen when an innocent person is dragged down into the pornographic sewer. And at the same time they deliver the message I want delivered: There is a way out.

The relationship is a win-win one, and that's the way any real friendship is supposed to work.

Just as knowing Gloria Steinem as a human being helped turn my life around, so knowing her as a writer helped turn the life of my book around. Gloria was watching *The Phil Donahue Show* when the woman in the audience wondered why feminists weren't involved in my cause.

Whether I personally knew anything about feminism or not wasn't important. In her writing, Gloria pointed out that my cause *is* very much a feminist cause: "Perhaps the unknown victims of sexual servitude—the young blondes of the Minnesota Pipeline, 'seasoned' by pimps and set up in Times Square; the welfare mothers pressured into legal prostitution in Nevada; the 'exotic' dancers imported for porn films and topless bars—will be the next voiceless, much-blamed women to speak out and begin placing the blame where it belongs. Now they are just as disbelieved as the rape victims and battered women were a few years ago."

No meaningful voice, no intellectual, had offered this kind of sympathy before. Gloria could have no first-hand knowledge of the world described in *Ordeal*, but still, she was able to understand it. And she seemed to understand what had happened to an overly sheltered, naive, gullible, frightened 22-year-old girl who had been dragged down into that world.

Gloria wrote a lead article about me in *Ms* magazine. Once Gloria's article appeared, an amazing phenomenon occurred. People started taking both my book and me seriously. Before then I had always been on the defensive, always explaining. As attitudes toward me changed, my own attitude changed. If someone lashed out at me, I lashed right back. And suddenly I was getting a brand new reaction from people: respect.

Gloria's article also drew a new kind of creature out of the woodwork; the intellectual critic who would never have otherwise noticed my book but now saw me as some kind of danger.

The biggest attack came from one of the editors of a publication called *The Nation*. His name, Aryeh Neier, and he put forth a theory that would have been hilarious if he weren't being so deadly earnest: Just as I had once been a captive of Chuck Traynor, used for his monstrous purposes, so was I now a captive of the feminists, being used for their monstrous purposes. "Lovelace is a great prize. *Deep Throat* is probably the most popular pornographic work ever. . . . The assumption that many of the women who perform in pornographic movies are coerced, as Lovelace was, serves a double purpose. First, and most obviously, it supplies an elusive link between pornography and actual harm to women; pornography becomes merely another manifestation of rape, appearing to justify censorship."

Neier's response to Gloria's article was all but unique. The main result of the article was that many thoughtful people picked up *Ordeal* and read my story in a way they might not otherwise have done. Suddenly I was reading the kind of responses I had hoped to get from the beginning— serious responses.

Such as a column by Judith Finlayson from the Toronto *Globe and Mail*: ". . . there's a very dark side to our sexual culture which Linda Lovelace experienced first-hand. All women should be horrified by the thought that 'respectable' men—even rich and famous ones—paid for the privilege of abusing the *Deep Throat* girl."

What I particularly liked about the new articles I was reading, even the Neier fiasco, was that the emphasis had been shifted. No longer was I the sole center of debate and argument. People had started asking questions of others, of the men who had abused me.

Here's Jill Tweedie, writing in the London *Guardian*: ". . . what no one questions or contemplates or gives any thought to at all, is simply this: never mind that Linda Lovelace did what she did—why, why, a thousand times why did her husband [Traynor] do what he did? Why did other men do what they did, with his contrivance?"

And Richard Cohen writing in the Washington *Post*:

"Whether pornography plays a role in violence directed at women is a question that for now can't be answered. But it's clear that at the least it's a raging insult to women. But so strong is the hold it has on the male imagination that when a book comes out by the star of *Deep Throat*, exposing it for the lie it is, the book fades from sight, while the movie plays on and on." Happily, the book *didn't* fade from sight, it hit the best-seller lists.

For the first time in my adult life, I began to appreciate the press. For now I was finally seeing the part of the press that didn't want everything pre-packaged and neatly arranged. Now I was running into people who were both thoughtful and concerned.

I was even beginning to relax a bit. There was hope, after all. People were listening to me and hearing me. They were understanding me and believing me. People were even buying my book. Royalties were accumulating and everything was just fine.

Right?

Wrong!

twenty-six

The minute the royalties started to appear, so did a figure from my past. This was Philip J. Mandina, a Miami lawyer who was once Chuck Traynor's business partner and later his lawyer.

Mandina was a major figure in my life. In some ways he has had as much of an effect on me as Chuck Traynor had. Long after Chuck disappeared from the scene, Mandina hung around, suing—and collecting—for back "legal fees." At this very moment—as I write these words—he's suing me for libel.

As soon as *Ordeal* was published, Mandina surfaced holding an old judgment against me—a piece of paper that seemed to entitle him to every penny I was going to make. While this is a complicated story, I'll outline it here briefly.

Ten years earlier, at the very moment I was escaping from Chuck Traynor, I had been scheduled to appear in a Miami nightclub with a live song-dance-strip act. Mandina was my attorney. He had arranged the deal and co-signed the contract, guaranteeing my appearance in a theater owned by something called the Ninth Street Amusement Corporation.

A few weeks before my scheduled appearance—when I was hiding from Chuck Traynor—it was clear I couldn't appear on the Miami stage, or on any stage. I called and explained to Mandina that I was hiding from Chuck and his guns and that he, Mandina, would have to explain that to the nightclub. When I didn't show up, the nightclub owner managed to get a judgment against me for $32,038.65 and now, more than a decade later, Mandina himself holds that judgment. Today, with interest, it comes to more than $40,000.

But you may ask: Isn't this a conflict of interest? An attorney represents me; the case goes against me; and now that same attorney winds up holding the judgment against me and collecting the money.

At one point Mandina flew up to New Jersey and called publisher Lyle Stuart's office; he announced that he was coming over immediately to look at the books and collect "his" share of the royalties. The unfairness of this was apparent not only to my publisher, but to a half-dozen of the men who worked in his warehouse. They decided they would give Mandina a somewhat warmer reception than he anticipated. However, he must have had second thoughts because he didn't show up.

However, in due times his process servers and legal representatives did show up and, in fact, started to collect my royalties. The unfairness of this and the apparent conflict of interest caused several prominent citizens—my new friend, Gloria Steinem, among them—to write the Florida Bar to petition for Philip J. Mandina's disbarment. Mandina assured the Florida Bar, "I did not represent Ms. Lovelace before or during her pornographic episodes, nor have I had any financial or professional interest in pornography."

The truth is that he did represent me in a great variety of ways and even drew up the basic Linda Lovelace Enterprises contract, one that guaranteed me three per cent of my income. And his fees were paid by Chuck Traynor's little pornography mill.

In deciding whether to disbar Mandina, the officers of the Florida Bar Association decided not even to investigate the information in *Ordeal*, and so Mandina's sleazy dealings with me—both sexual and financial—were ignored. The Bar confined itself to just one area: whether his possession of the judgment against me added up to *current* conflict of interest. The letter from the lawyer in charge of investigating Mandina was peppered with such phrases as "any literary license taken by Mrs. Marchiano in her novel [sic] *Ordeal*" and "I have no desire to allow this grievance to become a circus out of which Mrs. Marchiano can secure publicity for her book *Ordeal*."

These strictly limited disbarment proceedings had only one clear result. They forced Mandina to file a libel suit against me. How did this come about? Mandina was asked whether it was true—as my book had charged—that he had suborned perjury by helping Chuck Traynor construct an alibi for defending himself against a drug bust.

His reply: "Of course not." Asked what he intended to do about my book, he said, "I'm going to sue, of course."

And so nearly two years after *Ordeal* was published, Mandina launched his libel suit. Mandina told one of my publisher's lawyers that without the disbarment threat, he wouldn't have brought the libel action. At this moment, as I write these words, Mandina's libel action is pending.

Publisher Lyle Stuart was offered a chance to settle the suit for less than $15,000 and this was his response: "Not one penny!"

twenty-seven

Fighting the suit has cost Lyle Stuart more than $100,000 to date. But anyone who knows Stuart knows that he is a stubborn man, particularly when he feels injustice is involved. He went after both Walter Winchell and *Confidential* magazine, in their heyday, winning large cash settlements. When Stuart believes there's cause, he'll take the rubberband off his bankroll, and go all the way.

In order to defend ourselves against the suit, we had to do some checking into Mandina's background. Not much, really, just a little. Not much was necessary because Mandina's background is an open cesspool.

What I'm about to tell you is a matter of public record. But so far it has had absolutely no effect on Mandina's life. How can this be? How can a prominent attorney be found guilty of massive fraud and go on living a jetsetter's life untroubled by the Florida Bar, his crimes barely mentioned in the local newspapers, apparently untouched by the forces of justice and decency?

The story of Philip J. Mandina is peculiarly juicy, as intricate as any espionage novel. It involves grand larceny, tax dodges, a wealthy heiress, a call girl, a mastermind, and a cast of sleazy secondary characters that would make any TV writer drool. It's a story of unparalleled greed and unqualified villainy. Not exactly a whodunit so much as a how'dhegetawaywithit.

First, let me set the scene. Philip J. Mandina was suing me for libel, for what I told in *Ordeal*, supposedly because it had besmirched his flawless reputation. Or, as he himself worded it in his legal papers: "At all times mentioned herein, plaintiff has been a person of good name, credit and reputation in his profession, well known as an Attorney in the area of the City of Miami, Florida, for more than 18 years. Plaintiff was deservedly enjoying the confidence and esteem of his neighbors, of his colleagues in the legal industry [sic] and all others in the community."

Finally we were able to question this paragon of virtue, this "well-known Attorney in the area of the City of Miami." We were allowed to face him in a pre-trial discovery. Throughout an exhausting day, he did everything in his power to evade direct answers. His attorney, an ancient, chain-smoking, raspy-voiced Miami lawyer named J. Arthur Hawkesworth, Jr.—widely known as "Hawk"—constantly stepped in to tell Mandina to remain silent.

Time after time, Mandina flat-out refused to respond to the simplest of questions. Mandina wouldn't talk about former partner Carey Matthew's felony conviction. Or whether any grievances had ever been filed against him. Or whether he had ever been arrested. Or even what specific passages in *Ordeal* he found libelous.

And there was a question I would have *loved* to see him answer because I think the figure would astound everyone: "How much money have you collected from Miss Lovelace?" He refused to answer.

Again and again his response was, "I don't know" or "I don't remember."

Mandina's attorney, Hawkesworth, was as talkative as Mandina was silent and as obstructive as Mandina was noncooperative. Our attorney was Allen G. Schwartz, the noted former New York City Corporation Counsel. He outclassed Hawkesworth the way a purebred racehorse outclasses a milkwagon horse.

How would Mandina react when he discovered that we *knew* he had recently (and very quietly) been found guilty of massive tax fraud? And that finding had been connected to still *another* fraud, a personal fraud engineered against a wealthy client.

It seems that in 1982 Mandina was found guilty of filing a "false and fraudulent" tax return. The official name of the case—for anyone who cares to research it—is *Philip J. Mandina, et al. v. Commissioner of Internal Revenue, 43 TCM 359 (1982) (CCH) (US Tax Court 1982).*

The bottom line is that the Tax Court found that in 1969 Mandina had reported $637,925 less than he had made. That year he had declared an income of some $17,055 while masterminding the robbery of $2,600,000 from one of his clients.

The government found that while he was registering a total income of $17,055, Mandina came into possession of a $100,000 yacht (complete with full-time captain), a new Jaguar (to be followed shortly by a new Corvette), a motorcycle, an $86,585.60 home at Ocean Reef Club, and a private airplane. A man that can live this well on such a limited income is either extraordinarily thrifty or extraordinarily crooked.

Although there was a statute of limitations on stealing all that money from a client, there was no statute of limitations on the charges of tax fraud and conspiracy to commit tax fraud.

This may have been Miami's best-kept secret. None of this had appeared in the Miami *Herald*. Not a word has appeared in the Miami *News*. Here is how the information was presented to him at the deposition. At the end of that day tempers had grown short. Mandina and his elderly attorney were belittling, ignoring or ducking most of our questions.

After a brief recess, our attorney Allen Schwartz began again.

"Mr. Mandina," he said, "in paragraph nine of your complaint, you state, and I quote the paragraph, 'At all times mentioned herein, plaintiff has been a person of good name, credit and reputation in his profession . . . Plaintiff was deservedly enjoying the respect, confidence and esteem of his neighbors, of his colleagues in the legal industry [sic], and all others in the community.' Period, closed quote. Is that a truthful statement?"

"I believe so," Mandina said.

"Are there, to your knowledge, attorneys or courts which have found you to be a person of other than good reputation?"

"Not that I know of," he said.

"Do you know an attorney named Lawrence G. Lily?"

Lily is the name of the government prosecutor who successfully prosecuted Mandina for fraud. At this moment Mandina knew that we knew. He reached for a paper on the table in front of him and held it up to his face, hiding himself from his questioner. But there was no hiding from the questions.

"Yeah," he said, finally.

"Who is Lawrence G. Lily?"

"He's an attorney for the IRS."

"Does Mr. Lily, to your knowledge, believe you to be a person of good reputation?"

At this point, his lawyer, Hawkesworth, broke in with, "Ask Mr. Lily that, okay?"

"Ask Mr. Lily," Mandina echoed.

"Do you know a judge named Irene Scott?"

"Certainly," Mandina said.

"Who is Irene Scott?" our lawyer asked.

"She was a judge of my tax case."

"What was your tax case?"

"We are not getting into that," Hawkesworth hastily interjected.

". . . civil tax case," Mandina muttered.

"Isn't it a fact," Allen Schwartz was asking, "that you have been found, in a case before the United States Tax Court, to have been guilty of fraudulent conduct in connection with a conspiracy to defraud one Harriet H. Pierce of over two million dollars?"

"Don't answer that," Hawkesworth warned. Mandina's face is perpetually tanned, but as the line of questioning continued that tan seemed to be fading rapidly.

"Isn't it a fact," Schwartz went on, "that the tax court by Judge Scott held in a tax memo in 1982 that, quote, 'by clear and convincing evidence, the federal income tax returns for 1969 filed by Mr. Mandina were each false and fraudulent, with intent to evade tax?' Isn't that a fact?"

"Don't answer that," Hawkesworth said.

"Well, isn't that a matter that affects his reputation?" Allen G. Schwartz said. "Are you telling me, Mr. Hawkesworth, that I can't inquire as to matters in which Mr. Mandina was the subject, involving false and fraudulent activity and unethical conduct by an attorney? Are you telling me that is not relevant to his reputation in this litigation?"

"I didn't tell you anything," Hawkesworth said. "I told him not to answer it."

"If you tell me why, on the record, you are directing him not to answer it—"

"I don't think it is relevant or material to this case," Mandina's lawyer said.

"Mr. Mandina," our lawyer tried again, "did you in connection with a conspiracy to defraud one Harriet Pierce or Harriet Pierce Mitchell—"

"Counsel," Hawkesworth interrupted, "if you don't want to get off the subject matter of—"

"Wait. Wait. I haven't asked the question, because I am going to ask him a *lot* of questions about it."

"No," Hawkesworth said, "I am not going to wait. I am going to tell you now—"

"No, I am going to finish the question, please."

"Well, I don't think so," Hawkesworth said, turning to Mandina. "Let's go."

"As part of a conspiracy—"

"We are leaving, Counsel," Hawkesworth said. "Do you understand that?"

The question-and-no-answer session continued another

ten minutes before Hawkesworth and Mandina made good on their threat.

"Mr. Mandina," our attorney began again, "you have given to me earlier today, and in the response to interrogatories, a list of individuals, some of whom are judges, some of whom are former judges, some of whom are attorneys, as witnesses with regard to your reputation in this lawsuit. You recall those questions and answers, do you not?"

"Yes, sir," He finally answered a question.

"Have you discussed with those judges and lawyers the—"

"Get ready to go, I think, Phil," Hawkesworth said.

"—the matter included in the litigation before the tax court, including the matter relating to the conspiracy to defraud Harriet Pierce Mitchell . . ."

"Goodbye, Counsel," Hawkesworth said.

". . . of more than two million dollars."

"Goodbye, Counsel," Hawkesworth said. "Let's go, Phil."

"Let the record reflect that—"

"Let the record reflect we are leaving," Hawkesworth said.

So be it. Let the record reflect that at 3:05 on a hot Miami afternoon, the two of them, Philip J. Mandina and lawyer Hawkesworth, packed up their papers and fled the lawyer's office.

Clearly then, we were not going to get the facts about Philip J. Mandina from Philip J. Mandina. Fortunately, we don't have to. The facts about Philip J. Mandina—the kind of lawyer he is, the kind of human being he is—are easily available to anyone who wants to read through the transcripts of his recent trial for fraud.

And that same story was retold in his appeal, which was turned down by a Federal Appeals Court just a few months ago. Since he has chosen to be a thorn in my side forever, let me tell you precisely how he headed this conspiracy to defraud a client of nearly $3 million.

twenty-eight

First, the cast of characters. The Heiress—Harriet Pierce, multi-millionaire and heiress. The Bridegroom—Dana Mitchell, divorced father of seven, friend and business associate of Philip J. Mandina, and soon to marry the Heiress. The Call Girl—Terry Timme, friend of Philip J. Mandina, soon to be kept by Dana Mitchell (the Bridegroom). The Divorcée—Ruth Casey, restaurant owner, dupe in the first scam. The Attorney—Philip J. Mandina, attorney.

The nicknames may prove useful because this is a long and tangled story. It emerges from hundreds of pages of testimony, the record of *Philip J. Mandina, et al. v. Commissioner of Internal Revenue (1982)*. Although Mandina has several accomplices (also found guilty of fraud), he is the one given star billing.

The year was 1969. The Divorcée, Ruth Casey, owned a Miami restaurant known as Black Caesar's Forge. Regulars at the restaurant included a certain Dana Mitchell and a certain Philip J. Mandina.

Dana Mitchell wanted to buy the restaurant from the Divorcée. Not with his money, but with the money of the woman he planned to marry. She was the Heiress, Harriet Pierce, and she came up with $175,000, which she loaned to the Bridegroom's company, which eventually became known as DMI (Dana Mitchell Industries).

Oddly, the Heiress's money was deposited in a checking account under the name of Philip J. Mandina, the Attorney. Mandina then drew up papers establishing the firm bearing the initials of the Bridegroom, DMI. Mandina named himself corporate counsel for DMI; his private secretary and his private investigator were named as officers; the official DMI office was a room in Mandina's law offices. (This set-up was the same he later used in setting up Linda Lovelace Enterprises.)

DMI's first order of business was to buy the Divorcée's restaurant. This was done with four checks—one for $100,000, one for $50,000, and two for $25,000 each. All four checks were made out to Divorcée Ruth Casey, and she endorsed all four of them. However—get ready for the scam—she was allowed to cash only one, the $100,000 check. Mandina assured her she should be grateful to be getting that much. The other $100,000 in checks bearing her endorsement were cashed by . . . well . . . someone else.

According to court testimony, and to all outward appearances, the Heiress was very much in love with the Bridegroom. It's not just that she was often seen clinging to his arm. Her affection could be measured in numbers, large numbers, large round numbers. Because that same month, April of 1969, she was persuaded to invest some of her money in the firm that bore her Bridegroom's initials; she invested precisely $2,600,000 in DMI.

Although this would seem to be powerful evidence of affection, the Bridegroom was not content. He seemed to want more. According to another witness, Dana Mitchell didn't like the idea of starting out married life on a less-than-equal footing with his Heiress bride-to-be. Consequently, on the very day before the marriage ceremony, she presented him with a gift of $400,000. The Bridegroom accepted $100,000 in cash, and deposited that in his personal checking account. The other $300,000, in the form of a cashier's check made out to cash, was cashed by . . . well . . . someone else.

The Bridegroom's firm, DMI, made a loan of $100,000 to the Bridegroom, a loan that was never paid back. Of this amount, $97,000 found its way into Mandina's bank account. Supposedly, this was a combination loan and payment for the sale of a motorboat and a yacht. This enabled

Mandina to plunk down $93,000 toward an even newer and bigger yacht.

In August of that year, the Bridegroom signed a DMI check for $260,000. It was claimed that this money went into buying Sooner State Oil Co. stock, but, as it turned out, Sooner State was what is known as a shell corporation, an empty shell that looks something like a real business but is just a place to conceal money. The money dealings were all handled by a longtime Mandina friend and associate named Stefano Brandino, an Italian national who lived in the Bahamas.

And how did the Heiress's money disappear in this kind of a deal? Here's how. At a meeting in Mandina's office, Brandino bought 344,500 shares of Sooner stock for a reported $35,000. He immediately resold the stock to DMI for $260,000. Brandino was paid $3,000 for signing the right papers in the right places. And—poof!—more than $200,000 of the Heiress's money disappeared into thin air.

As complicated as all these dealings were, one thing became clear: Hundreds of thousands of dollars found their way from DMI into the pockets of the Attorney, the Bridegroom and two other partners. But this was a secret. They didn't want anyone to know that they were becoming rich while the Heiress was becoming poorer. Which must be why, when he filed his income tax form that year, Mandina reported an income of $17,055. The Bridegroom, on the other hand, didn't bother to file any income tax report at all.

Just a few weeks after the marriage, the Bridegroom, Mitchell, visited Mandina's yacht, where the Attorney introduced him to the Call Girl, one of two call girls who happened by on this particular evening.

This Call Girl's name was Terry Timme. It was love at first sight. The very next morning the Bridegroom asked the Call Girl to give up her profession. The Bridegroom immediately installed her in an apartment at the Jockey

Club and provided her with a $1,000-a-week allowance, a new car and many gifts.

The source for all this was, of course, the Heiress. The Heiress, then, was paying for her new husband's very own Call Girl. Naturally, the Heiress was unaware of this. All she knew was that the Bridegroom went off "to work" every morning at 9 a.m. and came home at 5 p.m. complaining about another tough day at the office. Of course, he was not really going to any office; he was going, instead, to the Jockey Club and spending a not-so-tough day with the Call Girl.

But then: Trouble. *Big* trouble! Dana Mitchell, the Bridegroom, found himself falling deeper in love with the Call Girl. In fact, he talked about leaving his wife, the Heiress (with her still-untapped millions), and running away with the Call Girl. When Philip Mandina heard this, he ordered the Call Girl to get to his office—and fast.

"Mr. Mandina at that time told me that he was in control of Dana Mitchell, and he would make any decisions whether Dana would see me or not," she testified. "He informed me at that time that he would also be paying me, not just Mr. Mitchell, and my job was to keep Mr. Mitchell happily married. And . . . he was telling me that Dana was working under him, and that he (Mandina) was running this whole show. I don't—at the time I didn't understand what he was talking about. And . . . he just told me I would take my orders from him, more or less, on how much time I would spend with Dana, and when I would see Dana."

"Did he indicate why you were to take orders from him?"

"He said he was running the show."

"What show?"

"At that time I wasn't aware of what it was."

"Did he make any reference to other individuals?"

"Yes," she said. "That was the time that he informed me that Dana's wife had the money, not Dana. He said Dana's wife had the money. . . . At the time he said there was a lot of money to be made, and what Dana was talking about was chickenfeed compared to what was the possibility, and I got the impression of a large sum of money at that time, but he did not put a figure on it."

One might conclude, therefore, that although the Heiress-Bride seemed to love the Bridegroom, he was not equally fond of her. According to the Call Girl that was, indeed, the case: "He married her for her money and . . . he wanted out. He couldn't stand the marriage but he had to stay until the shopping center was done."

Whoa, shopping center—*what* shopping center? The shopping center was the next stage in the plan to separate the Heiress from her inheritance. The basic modus operandi was the same as in the purchase of the restaurant. If you recall, there it was made to seem as though $200,000 was paid out when, in reality, the payment was only $100,000; the other $100,000 was unaccounted for. With a shopping center there were many purchases to be made and many numbers that could be inflated.

The Call Girl asked the Bridegroom what was so important about his shopping center.

"I asked him at the time why that was important, and he said because (of ordering) pipes and things, and they were to be a different price than what he ordered them for, and that's how they were going to take the money . . . say, if you would buy pipes at $10, and you would put down that you paid $20 for it. . . . This was what he explained to me, how they were getting money from the shopping center. He also took me and showed me where the shopping center was going to be built off 36th Street [in Miami]."

The Call Girl then reported that Mandina sometimes visited the Bridegroom at her Jockey Club apartment. At one of these meetings they discussed the purchase of a shell company—a make-believe corporation with no real assets, a device used to hide large amounts of money. The phrase "shell company" was not in Terry Timme's vocabulary, and her next response in court could be delivered properly only by an actress like Judy Holliday.

"They were talking about some money, and they brought up the shell company. I was not involved in the conversation. I was sitting back listening to the conversation. And Dana [the Bridegroom] was quite quiet, and the rest were talking about the shell company, and the reason it stood out so much is because I had mentioned it afterwards to a friend of mine when he asked what they were into, and I said they were into a gasoline station. I figured the Shell companies in the Bahamas were—they were going to have gasoline stations, and I was informed that a shell company is just the outskirts of a business that does not exist."

As quickly as possible, Mandina, the Attorney, found ways to steal Harriet Pierce Mitchell's fortune. Reading the trial transcript, I was reminded of an old Marx Brothers movie, people running this way and that with briefcases and paper bags stuffed with money, trying to find ways to hide it. Still and all, $2,600,000 is a lot of money to swindle.

One night a man came to the Call Girl's apartment with a briefcase full of money and it was her job to count it.

"How much money did you count?" she was asked.

"I counted over $200,000 that time."

"How much over $200,000?"

"I have—I keep putting this figure, $229,000 or $225,000, but I know it was at least $200,000, and I can't put anything more than that."

The money, most of it in $100 bills, was kept in the apartment until Mandina came over to collect it.

"The money was placed in a dresser beside the bed," she remembered, "and we stayed there all night, because of the money, and it was moved to Mr. Mandina's office the next morning."

"Why did you stay there all night?"

"To make sure nothing happened to the money."

Clearly then, Philip Mandina felt he had a very good thing going. And he was not about to let anyone or anything rock the yacht. But it wasn't enough to figure out what to do with all the money, he also had to figure out what to do with the people.

And the people were definitely becoming a problem. As Dana Mitchell, the Bridegroom, watched his new wife's money disappear, he began to develop a conscience. In fact, he decided to confess everything to his wife, the Heiress.

"He cried many, many hours," the Call Girl remembered. "Physically cried, and was very upset, because he wanted to go to Mrs. Mitchell and tell her what was going on, and get out."

"He wanted to go to Mrs. Mitchell and tell her what?" the judge asked.

"That he had made a mistake, and everything that had happened, and that he wanted out of it."

This would of course stop the flow of money into the pockets of Mandina. The Attorney was not about to let that happen. In fact, he got so upset with the Bridegroom that he refused to answer his telephone calls. The Call Girl was there when the Bridegroom tried, and this is the way she remembered it: "He would constantly call from the Jockey Club trying to reach Mr. Mandina, who refused to talk to him and told him: 'Stop being such a baby!' "

Mandina got very tough when he saw the Bridegroom getting cold feet. And once again he summoned the Call Girl to his office for a little talk.

"He told me that Mr. Mitchell had signed some papers," she remembered that meeting. "And that he would go to jail if he didn't continue where he was at. And that marriage was not involved in it, and that he could have me thrown out at any time, which I said I did not object to at that time. They also . . . they could stop saying he was at the office when his wife believed that's where he was every day."

Why would Dana Mitchell, the Bridegroom, sign papers that would get him in trouble? Because he had no choice. In a sense it was the same reason I signed every piece of paper that Mandina shoved in front of my nose. In fact, the Call Girl's sworn testimony rang more than a few bells: "Well, I know from my own experience that the three times that Mr. Mandina came with papers, Dana signed them without reading, and every time it was brought up, Mr. Mandina would tell Dana: 'Just sign the papers.'"

The Call Girl was then asked whether she had ever discussed the signing of papers with anyone.

"Only Mr. Mandina . . ." she said, "I remember going back to the day I was in his office, and he was making a comment at that time about he never put his name on any papers, when he was telling this other guy about this insurance company, and that he never put his name on any paper, so it could not affect him since he didn't put his name on it."

In 1980, when Mandina felt the hot breath of the tax people on his back, he tried to cover his tracks. He found Ruth Casey, the Divorcée, in Texas and asked her to sign a paper. Since she didn't have her glasses, he read her a paper aloud saying that she had received $100,000 for her restaurant in 1969; however, the paper she signed said that she had received $200,000 for the restaurant. The judge was not impressed.

According to the judge's summation: "Although the paper signed by Ms. Casey in 1980 stated that she had received $200,000 . . . her testimony at the trial was consistent that she only received $100,000. . . . We conclude that Ms. Casey was not completely aware of the contents of the document she signed in 1980, and in fact she only received $100,000. . . ."

In 1970, Dana Mitchell finally divorced the Heiress and vanished. Mandina tried to keep the operation going without him. In a sense, it became a family operation. His brother Jerry became president of DMI. Mandina even used his mother Margaret, a retired New York school teacher, as a front by sharing a safety-deposit box and a checking account with her.

The judge ruled that Mandina was part of a conspiracy here, but even if he weren't, it didn't matter "since the record clearly establishes that petitioners did have an agreement among themselves to extract money from DMI for their own benefit, and that they did so."

After all the testimony, the government was able to track down quite a bit of the money that had found its way into the pockets of Mandina.

In determining his real income during the year he declared $17,055, the court broke it down this way:

1. Partial proceeds of restaurant sale ($100,000) "diverted by you."
2. Check from Harriet Pierce ($300,000) "diverted by you."
3. Sale of stock in Sooner Oil ($225,000) "diverted by you."
4. Checks issued by DMI ($125,000) "diverted by you."
5. Partial proceeds of DMI checks ($98,000) "diverted by you."

And so on. Now I understand more fully why so little of the income made by me ever got to me. Because I was always surrounded and outnumbered by men like Mandina and Traynor, people skilled in the techniques of "diverted by you."

The judge—and later the appeals court—decided that Mandina somehow neglected to pay a "deficiency of income tax of $637,925." There is also a fraud penalty of $318,962. When you add the interest from 1969 until today, it might add up.

Philip J. Mandina continues to practice law in Miami, Florida. Both Harriet Pierce, the Heiress, and Linda Lovelace, the Porn Star, have had a share in paying for his practice. And we've both learned a very valuable lesson.

When I see how much was embezzled from Harriet Pierce, I shouldn't feel too bad. Compared to her, I'm small potatoes. The only thing that truly surprises me is that after all this, Philip Mandina has accused me of damaging his reputation.

twenty-nine

And so my royalties vanished before they reached my hands. "Diverted by" Philip J. Mandina. Though a best-selling author, I was poor again. Even while I was appearing on national shows and being written about in every leading magazine, our refrigerator was empty and our creditors were kept waiting.

But the book tour had to go on. Not just in America, but throughout the world. Maybe we hadn't exactly *conquered* America—but at least we'd made some inroads, along with some new friends. Now we were ready to tackle the rest of the world, starting with England and then going on to Scandinavia. The thought of going to Norway and Sweden stirred up just a few hobgoblins; ever since my days with Chuck, I'd heard Scandinavia described as the porn capital of the world.

But no longer did we feel so alone, so vulnerable. We had new friends in our lives, friends like Gloria Steinem. We had Lyle Stuart, a gutsy publisher who was backing us to the hilt. Having a friend like Lyle was a new experience for me; I never believed that any man, other than my husband, would be protective of me.

Still, leaving these shores has always been, for me, a

scary experience. The last time we'd been abroad was in the Philippines, the time I was fired from a film. I still remember the feeling of being in a strange hotel in a strange corner of the world without a friend to my name or a dollar in my pocket. And I'll never forget my happiness on getting back to this country.

Our new European tour started out very much like the tours back home with the usual round of press, radio and television interviews. However, this time there was a difference, a difference that existed within myself. It had much to do with the Gloria Steinem article and the other articles that followed. I was more sure of myself, more willing to speak up and speak out.

In England I ran smack into the traditional English reserve. During my first radio interview, I was (of course) asked why I didn't manage to escape from Chuck Traynor earlier. I must've been wound up because I exploded with the full answer.

"After our first day together, he began to beat me," I said. "I literally became a prisoner of his. I was never allowed out of his sight. I wasn't permitted to use the bathroom on my own. If I went into the bathroom, he came in with me. If he took a shower, I had to go in with him. I became totally embedded with fear. Each day was a matter of surviving, of trying to make it through that day.

"I made three spontaneous attempts at escaping and they were unsuccessful, needless to say. And I suffered a brutal beating for each attempt. And also some kind of sexual perversion for the punishment for having tried to escape."

As I went on painting what I felt was a true picture of unqualified brutality and terror, I couldn't help notice that my interviewer was betraying as little emotion as his microphone. So this was the famous stiff upper lip.

"What you are really saying then," he said, in clipped tones, "is that he *propelled* you into it?"

"Well," I said, trying to break through his reserve, "when

a .45 is put to your head, you find yourself doing strange things."

Another English reporter, Penny Perrick, took me on a tour of the SoHo sex shops. Although I'd been involved in pornography for years, I was only now getting an idea how big the business really was. Here was an entire section of London devoted to little else. Blinking neon signs saying, "Hard Porno!", windows decorated with dildos and life-sized blow-up dolls, magazines about whipping—the whole area was a museum of everything that's perverted.

Finally I stopped in front of a genuine oddity, an Italian grocery with a window display of drying noodles, imported cheeses and sausages, bottles of chianti. This, incidentally, was right down the street from something called the Anne Summers Sex Shop.

"If I owned this shop," I said to the reporter, "and that opened over there, I'd put a sign right here in the window asking people to sign a petition, some statement demanding that the other store be closed down."

Larry gave me a double-take.

"That sounds like a speech," he said. "Anyway, honey, we know it's never that simple."

But the reporter told me that many others felt the same way and that they were then in the process of banning sexually offensive window displays. I was pleased I'd had the courage to say what I felt.

"All this talk about freedom"—I was too far gone to slow down now—"why should people have the freedom to offend other people? All they really need is a sign on the door. Customers looking for that kind of thing have a sixth sense. They'll know what's there without any big display out front. It seems to me, if it's right there in the window, then it takes away some of *my* freedom."

"Yeah, I *thought* it sounded like a speech," Larry said.

As I was talking, the reporter was scribbling. Until that moment, I hadn't realized how much this kind of thing offended me. Why the strong reaction? Was it because these sexual artifacts reminded me of the past? Yes—but it went beyond that. I was surrounded by the symptoms of a sickness. No, not just a sickness, an epidemic.

Standing there in SoHo, I was surrounded by ghosts. At one time I had been neck-deep—throat deep—in this world. The 8-millimeter moviemaker who wanted the actors to urinate on each other . . . the still photographer who smeared ketchup over my back and then handed another girl a whip. . . .

Flashback to—

Lenny Campagno, a.k.a. Lenny Camp. South Miami, a living room filled with boxes and crates. Newspapers on the floor, cats crawling over everything, dirty dishes piled in the sink, cat hairs in the sugar bowl, a bed surrounded by floodlights, Lenny Camp telling Chuck, "Get her undressed now, tell her to take off all her things."

And Chuck saying, "Okay, Useless, get undressed, we're gonna to do some pictures here." And then producing another girl, Chicklet, no more than 18 years old but an old hand at this. Chicklet couldn't understand why I was crying so much.

Lenny Camp, two cameras roped around his neck, saying, "All right, girls, why don't we start off with a few kisserinos." Click-click-click. Me going numb, turning into a robot, feeling nothing as some skinny naked girl kisses me on the mouth and Chuck yelling, "Wouldja at least try to make it look natural?" (Natural? What could be natural about putting my hand on another woman's breast?)

Chicklet trying to calm me: "We'll just go through the motions together—you're gonna have to anyway—and then it'll be over with and you can forget all about it. Look, when you go down on me, just fake it. . . . I won't tell anyone." Go down on her? Oh, God! Then Lenny Camp coming in from the other room, strapping something large onto Chicklet, a make-believe male sex organ. Then she taking on the male role, getting on top of me and putting it inside of me. Click-

*click-click. A day of firsts. First still photographs. First dildo.
First female sex partner. The beginning.*

No. No more. Life was too short, far too short for these
ghosts.

I could feel a change coming over me. I had always
hated the porno world, but no longer was I going to keep
my opinions to myself. Why shouldn't I tell the world what
I really felt? After all, the world was listening now. I
decided not to pull any more punches, to let some of my
anger—no, some of my *hatred*—come out.

thirty

The reporter from *Now!*, an English newsweekly, asked me
what I *really* felt about pornography and I decided to *really*
tell him: "I would like to see people who read pornography
or have anything to do with it put in a mental hospital for
observation so that we could find out what we have done to
them."

Whenever I said something like that—something I really
felt or something that attacked someone—the pencils began
to move. So be it. That's what they really wanted and that's
the way I really felt—so why soft pedal my opinions?

The low spot of our London trip was a luncheon
arranged for us at London's Cafe Royal. I knew we were in
trouble from the outset. Somehow they had neglected to
tell us it was a formal affair. And Larry was dressed the
way he usually dressed, which is to say he was wearing
slacks, a shirt and a lumberman's jacket.

Before we got there, they had had the cocktail hour. In
fact, judging by the looks of things, they had had more

than one cocktail hour. All I knew is that everyone there—and this was supposedly the crème de la crème of London's literary establishment—was pretty well blitzed.

Beverly Hayne, feature editor of the magazine sponsoring the lunch, introduced me by retelling my story. As she told how I had been raped and beaten, her words got a reaction I'd never before seen. Most of the people in the room, most of these *literati* started giggling. At first they tried to hide their laughter but they were too blown away to do that with any success. Finally, every line she spoke got a bigger laugh than the previous one.

She tried to regain control of the meeting but it was useless. She said that Chuck Traynor had turned me into a "sex slave" and that he had used my body "as a credit card" and, for some reason, those thoughts got the biggest laughs of all.

If I had been smarter, I wouldn't have gotten upset; I would have just gotten out. I should have realized a couple of things. Most important, these people were so drunk that news of their mother's demise would have drawn a round of applause. Secondly, most of them hadn't yet read the book and they were still looking, through their bleary eyes, at the *old* Linda Lovelace.

"Hey, wait a minute!" I stood up and went to the microphone before the introduction was completed. "What's happening here? I can't believe you people are getting a *laugh* out of this. How would you like it if it were your daughter? What if this happened to *your* wife?"

I had to shout just to be heard and did. Finally the audience quieted down a bit. At least they stopped laughing. I was talking about the most alarming pornographic statistic I know—that the youngest known victim of child pornography was only 13 months old—and that seemed to start them laughing again.

At least one person there had read *Ordeal*. He was William Hickey, a *Daily Express* reporter. Hickey was later described in the London press as "a rude and objectionable fellow" and I think that's a splendid example of English understatement. Hickey, young and well groomed, got to his feet to ask the first and only question of the day.

"Oh, could you please tell us what happened to Rufus?" he said.

"You'd have to ask Mr. Traynor," I snapped.

My voice had a quaver in it. Rufus was the dog that Chuck Traynor once bought for the purpose of torturing me sexually. Several times Chuck had tried to bring the dog and myself together for publisher Hugh Hefner's delight. Rufus, needless to say, was a name that I wanted to forget.

I suddenly saw Larry get to his feet and walk over to Mr. Hickey. When they were inches apart, the reporter seemed to realize my husband was not fooling. I closed my eyes because I sensed Larry was about to knock this man out. Something had been happening to both of us. We had taken it long enough; we weren't going to take it any more.

"Do you feel better now?" Larry was shouting. "Do you feel a lot better now? Did you know that was the worst thing she ever went through and do you feel better now that you've said it? Why don't we talk about the Jews in the ovens and concentration camps of Germany, if that's the kind of conversation you really want to have?"

"B-b-but . . ." Hickey stammered.

"Why would you want to humiliate my wife?" My husband said to a room suddenly gone deathly quiet. "Would you like to go outside where we can talk about this?"

Hickey had no intention of going outside—or anywhere else—with Larry. At this point a woman on the dais tried to intervene: "Mr. Marchiano, would you kindly take your problem outside? I wish you would settle your grievance outside."

"Honey," Larry shouted back, "that's what I'm *trying* to do. I'm trying to get this dude outside."

"We're just here to have a good time," the woman said, apologizing to the room at large—not for Hickey's ill-mannered question but for my husband's entirely human reaction. "We're here to have a good time and I must say that I'm sorry about all this."

That was it for me. I got up to leave, but not before delivering a parting shot: "I feel sorry for all you people," I said. Then Larry and I just marched out. To the credit of the British press, in reporting the incident, the newspapers all seemed to take my side against Hickey.

Did we over-react to the Rufus question? It was the kind of question the former Linda Lovelace would be asked all the time. But both Mr. Hickey and I were a bit surprised to learn that she had been replaced. And the new Linda Marchiano wasn't having any of it.

Larry and I were coming into our own. By the time the story got back to the gossip columns here in the States, it was reported that Larry flattened Hickey in a brawl at a literary tea. The truth was somewhat less dramatic than that, but maybe more meaningful.

I think the two of us had developed some confidence, the confidence to stand up on our own two feet and *not* to be used or abused.

Norway and Sweden were directly ahead. There, the book was being published by small, independent companies that needed all the help my appearance could supply.

By the time we landed in Sweden, I was in a terrible mood. I hadn't been able to sleep in days and looked it. (Larry, on the other hand, had been sleeping easily and was well rested.) I was in a country where I didn't speak the language. Stepping from the plane and walking out into Scandinavian winter for the first time, we both realized we were inadequately dressed. Larry didn't own an overcoat and was trying to get by with a sweater. I was wearing moccasins.

We were met at the airport by two women from the publisher's office. One of the women showed me our schedule for the morning—three interviews over the next two hours, three interviews without a bite of food or a moment of sleep. I felt cold and tired—a combination of winter and panic. I went into my primadonna routine.

"Forget your schedules," I announced. "I'm not doing this tour. It's just too much and I'm too tired. I'm not staying here. Forget it, it's all over, get me a ticket on the next plane back to the States."

The publisher's representatives looked at each other, shrugged their shoulders, smiled at me and hustled me right along to the interviews. I'm so glad they didn't take my outburst seriously, because this was to begin the nicest two weeks I've spent anywhere.

At first I had doubts. The first day there was an autograph party at a major bookstore, and, much to my chagrin, only ten people showed up. There were other people in the store but not to buy books; they were there to study me out of the corners of their eyes. This was a frightening experience, another flashback; these were the same men who *used* to follow me. I could feel their eyes searching me out from behind the shelves of books.

We finally figured out what was happening. These people hadn't yet read any interviews or seen any reviews; the only Linda Lovelace they knew anything about was the *Deep Throat* Linda Lovelace.

Once they learned what my book was about, and what had really happened to me, a different kind of person came out. While in Sweden, I autographed 425 books in a single day—more than had been sold by a visiting Pulitzer Prize winner, or one of that country's leading television entertainers.

thirty-one

One of the first questions I was asked at my Swedish press conference was whether I blamed *all* men for what had happened to me.

"Not at all," I said. "It seems to me that we have many males in our society and very few men. Let me explain that. It seems to me that so many males are insecure—they can't treat a woman as an equal but must dominate them. A real man knows better. A real man can say: 'I'm a man and this is a woman and we are equals; therefore, we can share all things equally.'"

Within a day or so of our arrival in Sweden ten thousand copies of the book had been sold and the publishers went back to press for a fifth printing. That story was repeated in Norway. As I left both countries, I got the same report— there just weren't enough books to meet the demand.

When I received news like that about my past books, the fake books actually written by someone else, I'd feel embarrassed. This time I could feel good. And that good feeling was reinforced by meeting the people. At one stop I met four older women with numbers tattooed on their wrists; they were former concentration camp victims and they wanted to shake my hand.

"We beat the devil," they said as they were showing me their wrists, "and you did too."

The book cost the equivalent of $20 there and yet many people bought copies. It seems to me that different values exist in Norway and Sweden. Books are prized. And family life seemed to mean so much more. Go out on a Saturday or a Sunday and you'll see the mother, the father and all the children walking together.

The publishers saw what Larry was wearing and

promptly bought him a full-length, down overcoat. After seeing my moccasins, they bought me beautiful boots and a warm hand-made sweater.

The only problem in Scandinavia for me was the food they served in the middle of winter. The dried reindeer meat reminded me of beef jerky, except that it was ten times as tough. In fact, the high spot of the trip came the night we discovered a place called Michelangelo's Pizza Parlor.

But what does the food matter when the people are so nice? In fact, during our two-week trip, there was only one jolting experience. It could have been unpleasant—but we didn't allow it to become that.

I was in a Norwegian bookstore and there were lines of people holding books to be signed. Someone was counting, and as I reached number 182, I became aware of a person off to one side snapping my picture.

He seemed to be catching me at all the wrong moments, with my head down or my eyes shut and finally I decided to try and make it easier for him. I turned directly to him and gave him the kind of smile I was feeling that day, a smile as warm as the Norwegian people had been.

When the store manager thanked me for posing, I asked him where I might see these pictures eventually. He blushed a little, hemmed and hawed, and then said that the photographer was shooting the pictures for a leading pornographic magazine.

"I'm terribly sorry about that," he said.

"Oh, no problem," I said.

"No problem?"

"No problem at all," I said. "It's just that I won't sign another book until he gives me that roll of film."

"Oh, but surely . . ."

"No, I'm serious," I said. "I'm not moving a muscle until that roll of film is given to me. I definitely don't want my picture to ever appear in another porno magazine."

There was a long line of people—at least a hundred

potential customers—listening to this. When the proprietor saw that I was adamant, he tried to persuade the photographer to give me the film. The photographer explained through an interpreter that he didn't like the magazine any more than I did, but this was his job. At this point, Larry intervened. I could see that he wasn't angry, not really. But you would have had to know him very well to realize it was a put-on.

"How do you say 'cops'?" Larry asked in a loud voice and he was told. "Fine, tell him then we're going to call the cops and get the film back that way."

The photographer seemed unafraid; he explained that the police would do nothing; that Norway was a free country and people could take photographs whenever they wanted.

"All right, fine," Larry said, "then someone tell me how you say 'ambulance.'"

"Ambulance?" our interpreter asked. "Why would you want to say ambulance?"

"Because after we call for the cops, I want someone to call for the ambulance," Larry explained. "Because this dude is going to need an ambulance before he gets out of here."

Evidently the photographer understood a little English. Without waiting for the translation, he did a rapid vanishing act. Larry later assured me that he would not have struck him. Certainly not in a foreign country. And probably not at all. Larry was changing, too, mellowing out a bit, maybe maturing.

During one book-signing party, a man asked me to autograph the book to a specific young woman: "And would you please to write a special note. A personal note. She was going to come here today herself but she got scared. She has only been away from her pimp for two days—she saw you on the video and she decided to run away—but she is still too frightened to come out. I think she needs some of your strength."

My strength? That was such a new notion to me. But it was true. Every day now, as I saw how the world was responding to me, I felt stronger and stronger. This is the way I signed her book: "I hope this story gives you some of the strength it gave me. Let part of my strength go with you now."

This was not to be an isolated incident. Everywhere I go now I hear from girls or women who have suffered some of what I suffered. And, oh, my heart goes out to them. I guess that's when I find myself praying hardest of all. I can remember when there wasn't room for anyone else in my prayers; now my prayers are crowded.

Before we left Norway, there was a woman named Anita who wanted to meet with me. Anita was a prostitute who was trying to leave the business.

"What can I say to her?" I asked Larry. "What can I possibly say? How do I handle this? What can I give to this girl? How could I help her?"

"Don't worry about it," he said. "When you meet her, you'll *feel* what to say."

At first I didn't have to say a word. I just listened as an extremely attractive young woman named Anita told me her story. She had a small child, born out of wedlock, and she wanted to give her little boy what he needed, so she went out into the streets and worked as a prostitute. At the moment she was working as a cashier in a grocery store.

"Whenever my little boy needs something," she said, "I think about going back and being a prostitute. It's the only way I could ever get him something extra."

I asked her what choice the boy would make if *he* were able to choose for her. And I found myself talking to her about self-respect and strength, and how they have to go together—you can't have one without the other. I remembered what Victor Yannacone had told me and I knew how it had worked for me.

"Right now you've got your self-respect," I said. "It's one of the most important things in life. When you feel yourself weakening, look at yourself in the mirror. Look into your eyes and hold your head up high and smile and say to yourself, 'I'm a lady. . . .' "

Later I was sent a newspaper story about how one young woman gave up the life of the streets. Her name was Anita. In that interview she mentioned our meeting and she repeated that quote.

That's one of the big lessons I've learned from my experience. The most important thing you've got on earth is yourself and you've got to love yourself before you can love your husband or your son or your daughter or anyone else. I'm sure that's not too original—but to me, it was.

thirty-two

For the first time in my life I was feeling my own power. I wasn't waiting for other people to tell me what to do or how to behave. By the time we were through with *Ordeal*—through writing it and through talking about it—we had made quite a few discoveries about ourselves. Now I was following my own instincts, doing what I thought best. And perhaps that was the greatest reward to come from the book.

Strangely enough, once I was able to act independently, able to stand on my own feet and speak my own mind, I was no longer alone. Just as I began to feel that I could go it alone, that I didn't have to rely entirely on the help of others, that was the moment I began to get real help— meaningful help—from others. New friends were seeking me out.

In the past my support came from people who got paid for that support. If I had a problem, I called the lawyer or the plumber, the accountant or the electrician, and then, when the problem was solved, a bill arrived. Support cost me so much that, even with a great deal of money flowing in, I never rose above the poverty level. I drove a Bentley and wore expensive gowns, but I was poor. Some of the men in my life walked away with whatever was not nailed down. And me—poor little me—I did absolutely nothing to stop them.

Now, a different kind of friend. Who? Take Gloria Steinem as an example. When Gloria is in your corner, things get done. Should I find myself in legal difficulties and badly in need of advice, Gloria would travel several hours out to my little home and would bring with her a friend who just happened to be a lawyer. I have the feeling that if the pipes started leaking, she would have shown up with another friend who just happened to be a plumber.

Many of my new friends were associated with a group called Women Against Pornography. I had never even heard of this organization before and, if they had heard of me, it was only as an arch enemy, the biggest porn star of them all. "Look at Linda Lovelace" they were routinely told, "she *enjoys* what she's doing."

The minute I heard the name, Women Against Pornography, I wanted to join. Surely I qualified; what other woman had a better reason to be against pornography? The news stories about the organization described their headquarters as a small storefront office in a shabby section of Ninth Avenue, conveniently near Times Square. "Conveniently" because the group offered regularly scheduled tours through the pimp-and-prostitute centers, the porn shops and peep shows.

I neither needed nor wanted a guided tour of Times Square. But the more I read about the group, the more it interested me. I wondered what chance these women had against the princes of pornography, but I knew this was a fight I couldn't sit out.

Women Against Pornography—the idea made a great deal of sense. Pornography *is* a feminist issue. It's something men create for the pleasure of other men; the only role women have in it is as tool or victim. Porn exploits inequality and perhaps—who knows for sure?—it may lead to violence against women. The only people I ever knew to be directly hurt by pornography were women.

I know freedom of speech is one of our most important rights. I liked the idea that Women Against Pornography were not asking for restraint of speech; what they were trying to do was to educate people to the dangers of pornography. Instead of censorship, these women were calling for private action, such as the boycott of certain films.

I had only one question: Would they let someone who was once named Linda Lovelace join their group? The answer came from one of the group's two full-time organizers, Dolores Alexander: Yes. A strong yes. To say they welcomed me with open arms is to understate the case. One of the nicest days I have had throughout this experience was the day Women Against Pornography called for a nationwide boycott of *Deep Throat*.

Why is that movie still being shown? People do know the facts now. The horror story behind its making has been told in the major magazines, newspapers and on television talk shows. Although people know what happened to me, nothing has changed. The proof that I was beaten black and blue is right there on the screen. And yet, men still go to see it. The same holds true for the 8-millimeter movies which, if anything, were even more disgusting.

Finally, a breakthrough. At Yale University. *Deep Throat* was being screened by the Yale Law School Film Society as a combination fund-raiser and between-exams break. This seemed ironic to me. Yale is supposedly one of the best schools in the country. And Yale Law School is where so many of our future leaders and politicians are educated. I could understand some low-life fraternity at Podunk U.

doing something like this—but the Yale Law School?

But at Yale, something different happened. Suddenly leaflets started appearing around campus, leaflets asking people not to support the Yale Law School Film Society's showing of *Deep Throat*, leaflets answering many of the arguments people voice whenever I demand that that film not be shown.

The freedom-of-information argument: "Would you patronize a film society which showed movies made by white South Africans depicting the systematic exploitation and degradation of blacks—as entertainment? Would you go to a Nazi Night, a Klan Night, a White Supremacy Night?"

The what-harm-does-it-do argument: "You will be helping to finance an industry which in its mildest form perpetuates ideas of women as objects to be raped and humiliated and exploited, as well as being responsible for the production of 'chicken' porn (involving children five years old and younger) and 'snuff' films (in which the actual murder and dismemberment of women is filmed). You will be showing financial support for Chuck Traynor, who prides himself on having 'created' Linda Lovelace."

To me it was surprising—and moving—that a group of strangers would become involved in what I had always seen as my private fight. But the biggest surprise came when the Yale Law School Film Society cancelled the showing of the film. This was the first of several schools where the film was scheduled to be shown and then cancelled—because people cared enough to protest.

The next attempted *Deep Throat* boycott was on a larger scale. This was the attempted nationwide boycott, Women Against Pornography's way of welcoming a new member to the group.

I could see one advantage to having a Linda Lovelace join your group—it led to considerable press coverage. As New York *New* columnist Beverly Stephens saw it: "While Women Against Pornography has gotten some media attention, it took a name like Linda Lovelace to fill their office with reporters. . . . If an unknown porn victim or prostitute had told the same story, who would listen or care?"

thirty-three

On a dreary and rainy Saturday in late May hundreds of people formed a picket line outside the Frisco Theater in Manhattan, a movie house that had been showing *Deep Throat* for as long as anyone could remember. Since I was expecting a second child a month later, I wasn't allowed to participate. I didn't even see the pickets until that night on all the television news programs. And then I saw scores of women, along with quite a few men, carrying posters ("Deep Six *Deep Throat*" and "PorNo!") and marching in a ring outside the theater.

Immediately after the demonstration, I met with other women at the storefront headquarters of Women Against Pornography. Despite the fact that the small room was jammed with television cameras and reporters, I felt comfortable. Maybe because I knew I was surrounded by friends.

And among those friends was author-lecturer Andrea Dworkin, who introduced me.

"*Deep Throat* is not an expression of speech; it is a crime against this woman, Linda Marchiano, who, prior to and during the filming, was deprived of every human right guaranteed to citizens of this country. Those millions upon millions of men—especially those freedom-loving liberals— who found *Deep Throat* so much fun must be told what they should have known all along: that they have been enjoying and defending and laughing at the sexual abuse of a woman.

"I call on women throughout this country to rise up in fury against *Deep Throat*. Wherever and whenever *Deep Throat* is showing, a woman is being raped."

This day I was to meet and feel the support from many women who spoke every bit as powerfully. I was very impressed that actress Valerie Harper was there, as was author Susan Brownmiller and many other Women Against Pornography.

And then it was my turn to speak. This was a brand new experience for me. I had answered every conceivable question, but never before had I stood up and read words from a piece of paper. The tension of the moment joined with the heat, the crowd, the closed-in feeling, may have made me stumble a bit but I meant every word.

"My reasons for supporting a boycott of *Deep Throat* are personal, intensely personal. I hate the thought of people making money—and I'm talking about vast fortunes—from the most degrading and terrifying time of my life.

"What about you? What will your reasons be for boycotting *Deep Throat*? It seems to me there are plenty of reasons to choose from. What reasons? Well, you might consider boycotting the film on the simplest of grounds: basic good taste.

"Or perhaps you'll just decide to keep your hard-earned dollars out of the hands of men who brutalize women for a living. And there's the chance that you won't want to propagate an absurd but dangerous male fantasy—that some women get sexual satisfaction from being brutally throat-raped. Or maybe you'll just do it as a personal favor to me.

"If, however, you decide to see *Deep Throat*, I hope you'll pay close attention. And when you see those huge black-and-blue marks on my legs and thighs—believe me, you can't miss them—I hope you'll sense my pain and degradation; after all, you just bought a share of it."

Later, as the memorable day ended, I wondered whether it would do any good. The television cameras and reporters disappeared; the pickets packed up their signs; and *Deep*

Throat was still there as it had been ever since it was first released nearly a decade earlier.

However, a few months later—was it a residual effect?—the movie disappeared altogether from Manhattan. And today, as I write these words, it hasn't returned. Who can say whether that's a result of the boycott or not? Maybe a story like mine isn't accepted all at once; maybe it has to seep slowly into the public consciousness and then, after a length of time, it is gradually accepted. Perhaps *Deep Throat* stopped seeming so amusing so "chic," once people began to see I was telling the truth.

For me it was the start of something new. I began to feel that it was possible to change (if just a bit) the shape of the world. Larry was having trouble understanding what I was feeling. While I was giving the speech, he escaped to the crowd outside the headquarters building and waited for me to say my piece and head for home. He felt things had gone far enough; now was the time to put public appearances behind us and get back to the business of raising a family.

For me, an opposite drive. Although I was anxious to return home, there was too much unfinished business. It seemed the wrong time to retreat. For the first time I saw the possibility of victory. When all these people—both women and men—stood up on my behalf, it gave me something to stand up for, too.

And now, when Sigma Phi Epsilon fraternity at San Diego State University announced the showing of *Deep Throat* as a fundraiser, there was an uproar. Women told the fraternity boys that they would throw up picket lines and then carry their demonstration inside the theater. Some of the alumni warned the boys that showing the film would place the fraternity's financial future in jeopardy. The film was cancelled.

The war against pornography won't be won in a day or a year. However, individual battles can be fought and won. And there are other times when a loss can be as good as a victory. The real victory is education.

If a group decides to go ahead and show *Deep Throat*, no matter what is known about my victimization, what happens? What happens to the person who knows better but still goes ahead and buys the ticket? Is that movie something he is apt to enjoy? Or is it more likely that he will feel guilty and ill-at-ease? What is he going to feel when he sees the bruises all over my thighs? Oh, I think there is more than one way to register a victory in this struggle.

As I traveled to college communities, often just to speak out against a scheduled showing of *Deep Throat*, I made more and more friends. Friends like Kathleen Barry, author of the book *Female Sexual Slavery*. Before we got together—first to do a television program, later to speak before university audiences—I received a copy of her book. *Female Sexual Slavery* was Kathleen Barry's study of the ordeal of many women not unlike myself.

According to Kathleen, my situation was anything but unique: "Female sexual slavery is present in *all* situations where women or girls cannot change the immediate conditions of their existence; where regardless of how they got into those conditions, they cannot get out; and where they are subject to sexual violence and exploitation."

We were of the same mind—actually, of course, she is an intellectual and I've never been called that. But people like Kathleen Barry have been able to put my experience in perspective, to make it more understandable to myself and others. She knew more about me—more about women who have been through my experiences—than I did myself. And whenever she speaks about them, I learn a great deal about myself. And I just know she persuaded many women to at least listen to what I had to say.

"I have mentioned Linda Lovelace's name repeatedly and I get a very uncomfortable kind of response from feminists," she said during one speech. "She has come out with a strong statement regarding her enslavement, saying she was forced to do *Deep Throat* and a whole lot of hide-

ous and ugly things prior to that. When I read her book
before I met her, there wasn't a thing in it that surprised
me. It's an absolute confirmation of everything that's in my
book. . . ."

Addressing the Pittsburgh Conference on Pornography:
A Feminist Perspective, I found the theme I was to repeat
more than a few times.

"I often hear pornography described as 'a victimless
crime,'" I began. "I'm here to tell you that's a lie. During
the filming of *Deep Throat* I was a prisoner. I was repeatedly hypnotized, beaten, raped, tortured and threatened
with a loaded gun. Not for a minute do I feel I am the only
victim of this so-called 'victimless' crime.

"What about the films of sexual abuse of children five
years old or seven years old or nine years old—would you
dare tell me they are *not* victims? And does a person
become any less of a victim at age 11—or 13 or 19—or
ever?"

thirty-four

More and more often I was meeting people who saw things
my way. Many times I've been asked why I didn't sue the
men who used me. More than a few lawyers have explored
just that possibility. The statute of limitations prevented me
from suing the men who brutalized me directly; and the
men who continue to profit from showing *Deep Throat*, the
filmed record of that brutalization, seem beyond the reach
of any law.

That statute of limitations is a real obstacle to women
such as myself. After being enslaved and degraded for a
period of years, you don't just escape and go running to an

attorney. It takes years to get over the fear, to find yourself, to discover who you really are and what you're capable of doing.

One lawyer who became deeply involved in my life was Catharine (Kitty) MacKinnon. Kitty has remained a friend wherever she has gone. And she has traveled far and wide in leading the legal fight against pornography.

While an associate professor at the University of Minnesota Law School in Minneapolis, she persuaded the city council to pass an amendment to the city's civil rights ordinance, one that defined pornography as discrimination against women. The ordinance was co-authored by our mutual friend, Andrea Dworkin, who was also a visiting professor at the university.

This was important because it was the first attempt to use civil rights law in the war against pornography. And it was important to me, personally, because it would have given me some legal means of striking back at the men who imprisoned me and used me. And so when they asked me to come out to Minneapolis and testify on behalf of their legislation, it was my pleasure.

After an opening statement, I responded to questions from the City Council. One of the questions was the one that has always given me the most difficulty. But I decided I would handle that the way I'm handling everything else these days. I was asked again about the film with the dog. The chairman gave me a possible out—"Would you like to respond?"—but I didn't want any more outs; I wanted to face up to it all. Finally, I *had* to face up to it.

Flashback to—

The gun. A revolver. Sitting on a small table. Surrounded by three men. And Chuck threatening me: "This is direct disobedience to a fucking order. You know the only choice you got? You make this movie or you're going to die. That's your big choice. . . . Take off your clothes, cunt." Three men and one gun—what chance did I have? Reaching up then, unbuttoning my blouse, surrendering. Oh, God! A dog. An animal.

Me, naked, on a mattress, and the director saying, "Now look around the room. Slowly, slowly. Now you see your dog and you go 'Oooooooh!' and now you look excited. Make it look like all of a sudden you're coming up with a brilliant idea. That's right, now snap your fingers."

And then the dog, tan-colored dog with short hair, longer than a German Shepherd but skinnier. And the dog's owner, a young man in his mid-twenties, saying, "This old fellow can go all day and all night. Don't sweat it."

The glare of the lights. The dog's eyes glittering, beady, in those lights. "Okay, Linda, now pet the dog. That's right, pet the dog. . . . Okay, now we'll try a little foreplay. How's the dog with foreplay?" "Just sensational is all," the owner says. The dog licking me then, licking me all over. "C'mon, Linda, laugh it up, you're supposed to be enjoying this! That's right, laugh!" Laughing hysterically but wanting only to cry. "Okay, Linda, now get down on all fours. That's right . . . Wow, this fuckin' dog is game, he's game for more. Lookit him go—we got a real winner here. Nice dog, good doggie."

The men giving the dog a biscuit, petting him. Chuck staring at me, studying, measuring. He knew, he knew this was the worst moment of my life and he would use it against me forever. For me there were no more humiliations, no greater degradations, nothing that would ever feel worse.

"Yes, I think it is important that everyone understands," I said. "Prior to that film being made, about a week, Mr. Traynor suggested the thought that I do films with a D-O-G and I told him that I wouldn't do it. I suffered a brutal beating, he claims he suffered embarrassment because I wouldn't do it.

"We then went to another porno studio, one of the sleaziest ones I have ever seen, and then this guy walked in with his animal and I again started crying. I started crying.

I said no, I am not going to do this and they were all very persistent—the two men involved in making the pornographic film and Mr. Traynor himself.

"And I started to leave and go outside of the room where they make these films and when I turned around there was all of a sudden a gun displayed on the desk. And having seen the coarseness and callousness of the people involved in pornography, I knew that I would have been shot and killed.

"Needless to say, the film was shot and still is one of the hardest ones for me to deal with today."

It was a relief finally to be able to talk about it. The questioning went on but the other questions didn't bring old ghosts back to life. I was asked about something that was very much on my mind.

"How do you feel about the existence of the film *Deep Throat* and its continually being shown?"

"I feel very hurt and very disappointed in my society and my country for allowing the fact that I was raped, I was beaten, I was put through two and a half years of what I was put through. And it's taken me almost ten years to overcome the damage that it caused.

"And the fact that this film is still being shown and that my children will one day walk down the street and see their mother being abused, it makes me angry, it makes me sad. Every time someone watches that film, they are watching me be raped."

The questioning was over and it was time to leave. But I had something more to say.

"Thank you," I said. "I would like to say thank you for everybody who made it possible for me to be here tonight. I want to speak out for what happened to me and for other members in our society. I feel that it is important that victims have a chance today in our society. And I also want to say that my children thank you."

The ordinance was passed in Minneapolis, only to be later vetoed by the mayor. The issue, however, is not a dead one. The same drama is being played across the country—even in my own home county in New York. When they asked me to speak on the legislation there—it was almost the same as the one proposed in Minneapolis—I agreed, but with reservations. This was too close to home and I've tried to avoid notoriety in the quiet community where I am now bringing up two small children as normally and peacefully as possible.

My life suddenly had a purpose. If anyone was doing a story on pornography, I was on the list of people to see. And that was just fine with me. If they can use me, I'm happy to be used for something worthwhile.

The people I've met in this fight, and the people I continue to meet, strike me as independent and smart. And, on occasion, just a bit scary.

Larry was not happy with all the women who were suddenly my friends. But this part of our life has been an education for both of us. Some of these women are quite tough. Larry makes jokes about how tough they are. But the way I look at it, to survive in this world, you have to be tough.

If these women didn't always remind Larry of the old-fashioned girls and women, that's too bad—but at least no one is using them. However, there was one who made us both a bit nervous. Although we were fighting the same war, we had different battle plans.

She felt that education and legislation were too slow and unsure. Direct action was her answer. She thought nothing of smashing windows in a book store or throwing a Molotov cocktail into a porno theater. (I happened to meet her in a small town where the fire department was on strike and she said, "Oh, wow, now's the time I should get into business again.")

Over the past couple of years I've gotten other letters from her and now she feels she was too radical. The last letter I got from her, she was settling into the community and trying to get back her children from her former husband.

I'm still bothered by the pornography-fighters who are too impatient, too radical. On the one hand you've got the extremist, the bombthrower, and then you've got the women like Gloria who go about everything through legal channels. I guess the Blacks had the exact same problem with their Panthers and the NAACP.

While I hate pornography as much as anyone, I think it should be fought through proper channels. I don't think violence is necessary. The business of busting up windows and bookstores and theaters is wrong.

Often these days I'm asked what should be done about pornography. I don't think I should be the one to say. The truth is this: I don't really know. I can describe the problem; I can tell about my experiences; but I'm really not qualified to give the solution to that problem.

It seems to me that recently they've been taking a very creative approach to the problem in California. People have always had trouble defining such terms as "pornography" and "obscenity" and "lust" and without precise definitions, there can't be much of a law. The other major roadblock is trying to find a law that doesn't interfere with freedom of speech.

A 1982 California law simply outlaws the hiring of a person to perform a sex act. If it could be shown—as it clearly could be—that I had been hired to perform sex acts in *Deep Throat*, the culprits might have been punished.

In a recent test case the defense claimed that the women were actresses and, thus, protected under the First Amendment. The jury, given a chance to see the movie, decided they weren't actresses after all. And the verdict was guilty.

Many people feel this is a basic moral issue and they're going to take extreme measures. I can understand that. I don't think *Deep Throat* should be playing in any theater at all, not anywhere in the world, and knowing that it is makes me feel a little desperate from time to time.

Sometimes I wonder whether all the talking makes any inroads at all into the porno business. When I'm in a depressed mood, I doubt it. Those darkest times usually come late at night and I wonder how many people are watching the movie at the very moment and how many of them have been intrigued by the knowledge that I was an unwilling participant.

But who can really tell what the result of all this is? When I'm in a strange city doing a phone-in radio show, there will always be calls from men saying they had no idea, that they would never again go to a porno movie. I don't doubt their sincerity. But does it really hurt the porno industry? Probably not. Maybe the porno business is a rhinocerous and I'm just a BB pellet bouncing off it.

But for me, personally, it has had tremendous meaning. The bad experiences I had to go through have value, and a life that once had no meaning now has some meaning.

thirty-five

All those people who terrorized me and haunted my nightmares—where are they now? It has been many months—make that years—since I've awakened to find those five nightmarish figures surrounding my bed. The ghosts have been exorcized and the flashbacks are rare. Finding the strength to deal with yesterday has given me the strength to deal with today.

And now, when the old villains do reappear, it is as real people, not ghosts. And once I see them as human beings, the fear dissolves.

One person who always manages to surface is Chuck Traynor.

As I mentioned earlier, Mandina is in the process of suing me for libel. The section of *Ordeal* that caused him the biggest problem was my account of being in his office when he and Chuck constructed an alibi that would explain why Chuck was found carrying bales of marijuana to his car.

Attorneys are not supposed to help construct false alibis—it's called "suborning perjury"—and Philip J. Mandina had to demonstrate that I was lying about this incident. He needed a witness, someone who could, and would, verify his version of the story, a person who might serve as both eyewitness and character witness. Whom did he choose? None other than Chuck Traynor.

The day before taking a solemn sworn statement from Chuck, the two men met in Las Vegas and talked the whole thing over. I want you to keep in mind one thing: This is Philip J. Mandina's serious attempt to demonstrate that he is not the kind of person who would ever "suborn perjury."

From the beginning of his sworn testimony, Traynor suffered peculiar memory lapses. When Mandina asked him the name of the lawyer who represented him in his drug-smuggling trial, he couldn't recall the name Carey Matthews (the convicted felon who is Mandina's former law partner), even though Matthews also happened to be Traynor's former commanding officer at Fort Bragg.

Another strange memory lapse came when he was describing the day that he and a confederate picked up the bales of marijuana dropped onto an empty field from an airplane piloted by a friend. (According to the alibi worked out with Mandina, the two men were scouting terrain for a parachute club's jump zone and just happened to stumble across the marijuana.)

"We didn't know it at the time," Traynor swore in his deposition, "but it was a drop zone for smugglers . . . deer hunting season had opened at that particular time and there were deer hunters, and we discovered these bales of marijuana and proceeded to carry them out to the road and got arrested carrying them out to the road, and charged with smuggling."

"Who was the gentleman who was with you at the time?" Mandina asked.

"You know, it's been so long ago," Traynor said, "I'm terrible about names. His name was—"

"Well, if you don't remember—"

"I can't remember," he said.

Mandina then brought up the book *Ordeal* and asked Traynor whether it was a true story or not.

"Have you ever hypnotized anyone?" Mandina asked.

"Hypnotized anyone?" Chuck repeated.

"Yes."

"No."

"She indicates in the book that you hypnotized her. Would you comment on that?"

"Yes," Chuck said, "I read that in the book. Hypnosis—"

"The question is, really, did you ever hypnotize her?"

"No," Chuck said.

Why would Traynor deny that under oath? So many people know the opposite to be true. Of course, he hypnotized me. Repeatedly. In fact, Chuck told an opposite story to *Screw*: "Marilyn Chambers and I did talk at the Flamingo Hotel in Las Vegas before the American Institute of Hypnosis. Twelve hundred doctors and they were very interested in what we did because doctors always use hypnosis negatively. . . . They would say, 'You *do* feel it. It's extremely pleasureable. . . . The doctors were very interested in my technique." At that same time Chuck was asked whether he had used hypnosis on Linda Lovelace, and he said, "Oh yeah."

Back to the Mandina-Traynor sworn statement.

"Well, first of all, she indicates from the beginning of the book throughout her relationship with you, that you kept her in fear of her life. What about that?"

"Well, it's totally untrue," Traynor said. "It's kind of a joke."

"No, never," he said.

"Do you know of instances where Miss Lovelace was

forced by you or anybody else in your company to do anything she didn't want to do?"

Of course not. Of course I *wanted* to do that sword-swallowing routine on a half-dozen different men in *Deep Throat*, I *wanted* to have a professional sadist torture me with a hair dryer, I *wanted* to do things that no human being would ever want to do.

(Chuck provided a more accurate description of our relationship during a tape-recorded interview with *High Society* magazine: "First of all, I'm very possessive. Secondly, I'm probably a lot more physically capable of threatening people than most. Of course, if you care about somebody and if you're involved with them in the film business and they say they are going to leave you, I think a normal reaction would be, 'You better not or I'll bust your ass.'

"I just would not say to anyone involved with me professionally or emotionally, 'Yeah, you can walk out the door anytime you want to.' Whether I would or wouldn't 'bust their ass' would depend on the particular situation.... I would tell her not to leave, probably forbid her to leave, just as I imagine most boyfriends or husbands or managers or pimps from the South would do.")

Then Mandina asked him about the section of my book dealing with Sammy Davis, Jr. In *Ordeal* I had described the nights we spent with Sammy and told of the many times I was ordered to satisfy the entertainer orally.

Here's Chuck under oath: "We went over to dinner there several times and ate with Sammy and his wife. We attended his shows in Las Vegas and New York. There was not any sexual association with any of us, you know, we were just friends."

I imagine even Sammy would roar at *that* description. We never went to one of Sammy's shows in New York or Las Vegas. And the rest of it is just as false.

Then Mandina asked Traynor to describe my encounters with a dog for the viewing pleasure of *Playboy* mogul Hugh Hefner. How would Chuck describe our relationship with Hefner?

"He's an art film historian and I helped him along those lines for a few months. Again, there was never anything—Hefner, he himself, was never overly interested in her. He saw her on a couple of occasions, that's about all there was to it." I'm sure Hefner, that old art historian, must be smiling as he reads those words.

"Mr. Traynor," Mandina asked at one point, "have you ever been convicted of a crime?"

"No," he swore.

In point of fact, I have a copy of an arrest—and conviction—record for a certain Charles Traynor. But why go on? Clearly, Chuck Traynor lies about as easily—and almost as often—as he breathes.

Whenever I visit a foreign country on a book tour, I'm always asked what jail Chuck Traynor is in. When I explain that he is still free and doing what he has always done, people stare at me. How can that be? How can a human being do all of the things he has done and not be in prison?

I explain this as best I can. I explain about the statute of limitations. I say in our country a man can do almost anything he wants to his wife and the police are reluctant to intrude. I explain the difficulty in launching a lawsuit in this country unless you have a lot of money or happen to be a lawyer yourself. A poor person doesn't have much of a chance of getting a good lawyer's services.

Finally, I am no longer afraid of Chuck Traynor. Maybe that's not entirely accurate. Maybe there's just a bit of wishful thinking attached to that statement. But at least the fear is fading. I no longer look fearfully for his face when I walk down a street; I no longer expect him to confront me with his semi-automatic .45 in his flight bag.

thirty-six

I assume that Chuck Traynor and Marilyn Chambers have the same kind of relationship that we once had. (I see she has even been linked to Sammy Davis, Jr. Her quote: "I'm not romantically involved with Sammy. We're just good friends and business partners.")

Happily, however, these days I am far removed from their world. I only assume that it would be easier for a skunk to become a poodle than for Chuck Traynor to change his ways.

Whenever Chuck and Marilyn are being interviewed together, the reporter notices something amiss. Reporter Joyce Wadler was one writer who happened to see Chuck both with Marilyn Chambers and with myself. She emphasized the similarities while covering Marilyn Chambers' speech at a college for the New York *Post*. This was long before *Ordeal* was published and before the public knew my true story.

"Miss Lovelace and Traynor had a very close working relationship. Miss Lovelace refused to do interviews without him. She looked at him before she answered questions. Often, she didn't answer questions at all—Traynor answered for her.

"Yesterday, it became apparent that Miss Chambers and Traynor are also working very closely together. Chambers does not want to go anywhere without him 'for security reasons.' She looks at him before she answers her questions. And sometimes, fairly often, she doesn't answer questions at all. . . .

"Then someone in the audience of 250 asked Miss Chambers what the difference was between her and Linda Lovelace, and Traynor said it was a question of direction.

"Finally a woman student attacked Traynor for answering for the entertainer.

" 'We work very close together,' said Miss Chambers. 'I like being dependent on men. I am an old-fashioned girl.' "

"Old-fashioned girl"—isn't that pathetic? In Chuck Traynor's vocabulary, an old-fashioned girl is one who allows herself to be pushed around and brutalized by men.

And that business about liking to be dependent on men—these days that really bothers me. If I were not so dependent on men, if I had not been such a dependent personality, I might have avoided ever meeting a Chuck Traynor. I don't think anyone should be totally dependent on anyone.

But I had been brought up to believe that I was supposed to have a man around and a man was supposed to take care of me. A man was something to cling to, to identify with, to obey. Now I know different. You have to be an individual first and then if you want someone else around, fine.

My biggest mistake—until recently, really—was letting whatever man I happened to be near make all the decisions, no matter how bad those decisions were. And there's a reason for that. I've spent a lot of time trying to get in touch with myself. And so long as the man wasn't beating me, wasn't handing me around to his friends, I would happily let him make all the decisions. Some of these decisions eventually cost me hundreds of thousands of dollars.

If Marilyn Chambers is reliving my experience, how can anyone help her? I don't know. One who tried to help was (unsurprisingly) Gloria Steinem. Concerned about Marilyn's safety, Gloria sent her a message that help was available. The message was carried by Seattle *Times* columnist Erik Lacitis.

When Marilyn Chambers heard about Gloria Steinem's offer to help, she laughed: "Well, you can tell Gloria Steinem that I am a totally healthy human being. Linda Lovelace is full of it. I am not scripted in anything to say.

People like Gloria Steinem ought to use their vibrators a lot more, especially if they're so damned frustrated sexually."

Lacitis then asked whether it was true that Chuck Traynor was always hovering around her.

"No!" Marilyn Chambers said, then cited an example of her independence. "He left for a couple of hours the other day . . ."

Then, with Traynor present, Lacitis repeated a series of questions that Gloria Steinem wanted answered.

Q—Was Chuck Traynor acting as a pimp? Does he now or did he possess guns? Does he threaten people with guns?

Traynor's answer: "I have never acted as a pimp. I am a gun collector, I have quite a large collection. . . . I don't threaten people with guns." (When *High Society* asked, "Were you ever a pimp? Did you ever have women fucking and you get a piece of the action?", he had a different answer: "Yeah, I had a business like that at one time.")

Q—Why is Chuck Traynor always making a living off another person who happens to be a woman? Why doesn't he work on his own?

Traynor's answer: "I don't make a living off anybody. I create women. Linda Lovelace, when I met her, was making nothing. My job as a manager is to manage female sex stars. If I stop managing them, they stop making money."

Q—What about the incident quoted by columnist Larry Fields, the time Marilyn had to ask for permission to go to the bathroom and you refused to give her permission?

Chambers's answer: "First of all, Larry Fields, or whatever his name is, is a hypothetical name [*which should come as a surprise to Larry Fields*]. I've never had an interview with anybody like that in Philadelphia. . . . Anyway, if Chuck ever said it, it's because I had to go onstage soon, and I should have been smart enough to go to the bathroom before. I deserved it. . . . I personally enjoy being submissive. I don't ever want to stand up to a man like

Gloria Steinem does. I enjoy a guy who is the boss."

Q—Would Marilyn Chambers allow Gloria Steinem to interview her alone?

Chambers' answer: "I'd never do anything without Chuck around. I don't feel safe around someone like Gloria Steinem. How do I know that she's not going to kidnap and take me away? I think that her problem is that a lot of these women libbers are too ugly to even get a man who'd want to be in charge of them."

Q—How would she describe Chuck Traynor?

Chambers' answer: "You know, Chuck is pictured as this creepy guy. He's not. He's one of the nicest men I've ever met in my life. . . . Do you know that I can't pick out what kind of clothes to wear for an interview? Chuck himself picked out these clothes. . . . I rely on Chuck for everything, absolutely everything at all. I know that I need it. I know that I am not really good on my own. I need Chuck. I need guidance."

There is a kicker to this series of events. In a subsequent interview with a men's magazine, Marilyn Chambers referred to the Lacitis interview. She said that the notion that she might be a prisoner was absurd; that, in fact, the message from Steinem had been delivered to her with Chuck Traynor gone; that, moreover, he hadn't been with her for several days; that, in truth, she was on her own. Which would have been interesting if true; however, Traynor was in the very next room when Lacitis delivered the message and he joined them immediately.

The relationship between Chambers and Traynor is clearly one of total dependency—whether that dependency is maintained through brute force we won't know until the two of them are apart.

thirty-seven

Despite the obvious lies in his deposition to Mandina, Chuck Traynor no longer bothers to deny that our relationship was basically a brutal one. And that fact, the basic fact of *Ordeal*, has been substantiated by more than a few witnesses.

A few years ago in a syndicated column by Marilyn and Hy Gardner, Chuck was asked what I was like when he first met me. Here he told the truth: "She was better at housework and cooking than sex. She was a lousy lover. When I first dated her she was so shy, it shocked her to be seen in the nude by a man." In England's *News of the World*, Traynor talked about our first days together: "She was frigid in bed and even kept her curlers on at night. She wouldn't undress in front of me because she was too shy. She was better at housework and cooking than sex, about which she was most unimaginative. . . . She often used to cry and tell me she had hardly any previous sex experience."

And here he is in *High Society*: "When she got involved with me, she got involved with that lifestyle. But at any time *in those early stages* [italics mine] she could have walked away. In her book she indicates from the very first I captured her and that was it. That's a bunch of shit. First of all, there were ten or twelve girls who were a helluva lot better looking than her. . . ."

In that particular interview, Traynor set several records straight. Here he answers the question of whatever happened to all the money that Linda Lovelace earned: "She got the money and gave it to me. That's probably the way it came down."

The part I liked best is when they asked him about beating me. To Mandina and others he denies that ever happened. Here he skates closer to the truth!

"I was raised in the country and I still live in the country," he explained. "I don't consider it beating if you slap your old lady for something. To me that's almost a sign of feelings, of closeness. When your old lady does something wrong or when she's giving you too much lip or something—I don't really consider that beating up."

In many interviews, Traynor also admitted that I had nothing whatever to do with the writing of the quickie-cheapie book under my name: "I wrote the book *Inside Linda Lovelace* with another guy before Linda and I split up," he told Hy Gardner. "The book and its theme were totally my idea. I created all the sex situations in it, just like I created Linda Lovelace."

Incidentally, Traynor also makes a liar of Mandina. Mandina has denied that anything sexual ever went on among us. In my book I had described the time Mandina telephoned us on the West Coast to get some eleventh-hour deep-throat instruction for his girlfriend.

Chuck has told the same story to *Screw* magazine: "A funny thing happened one night in Malibu. The phone rang, it was a friend of mine, an attorney, in Miami. A young guy, you know, and he's got a girl who's been seeing him for several years, and he called me up and we were casually talking about one thing and another and he said, 'Say, Chuck, about that deep-throat thing, how do you do that? How does Linda do that?' And I said, 'She lays on her back and puts her head back to elongate her neck.' I didn't tell him about the hypnosis because he didn't ask. . . ."

Again, in this interview, the subject of beating me came up. You'll remember that Traynor, under oath, denied to Mandina that he beat me.

"I wouldn't bullshit anybody," Traynor said to *Screw*. "I've always tried to deal with people two ways: I talk to them as long as I think I can talk to them, and then I hit them. With Linda, you know, if she and I got into a hassle, it wouldn't be beneath me to backhand her or bend her over my knee and beat her ass. Linda dug it, you know."

Ladies and gentlemen of the jury, I rest my case.

In going over all of his statements about our life together, I see one thing more clearly now than ever before. I describe life with Chuck as twisted and brutal, demented and violent, insane and sadistic; he describes it as normal—believe it or not, we're both telling the truth.

Traynor is the one responsible for the creation and marketing of Linda Lovelace. Over and over again, he told reporters, "She was nothing, nothing—I made her everything she was."

At times his pride of creation takes an almost humorous turn. As when he was speaking to investigative reporter Martin Yant: "I *did* create Linda Lovelace. That's what burns me up almost more than anything else. I gave her a real opportunity. There are hundreds and thousands of girls who would have loved to be in her place and *this* is what I get in return."

Many seem to think that I'm at least partially to blame for what Chuck was able to do to me. I hear conjecture that perhaps I am a "natural victim," a masochist who thrives on abuse.

I know better. I'm a person who thrives on affection and love, on being with decent people who behave decently toward each other. And I don't believe there was anything within me that caused Chuck to suddenly act this way. In fact, I know otherwise.

One of the nicer byproducts of my book, *Ordeal* was that it brought me into contact with many people who have had similar experiences. One was more than just similar, it was identical. For one of my correspondents, now a close friend, was the woman who lived with—and escaped from—Chuck just before he got hold of me.

At this point, I won't reveal her first or last name. The truth is, she is still terrified of Chuck and fearful that he'll discover where she lives or what she is doing. I will just say that she's a university graduate, a professional woman, charming and lovely and intelligent.

She was fortunate enough to escape—she ran off leaving all her belongings behind—but she still lives in absolute dread of Traynor. She, too, was once taken by Traynor to Mandina's office: "When I met the attorney for the first time, he looked me over and said something like, 'Is she your newest one?' And I thought he meant girlfriend!" She saw the same thing I did—both men knew that Traynor was guilty and both were working together on the construction of the defense; at that time: "Their approach was going to be illegal search."

In one letter, she mentioned her thoughts of escape: "When you wrote of watching the door on occasion, in hopes of escaping, it brought back the feelings I had had several times. It would be quiet in the house and I would look at the door briefly. Then, from out of nowhere, Chuck would walk into the room. It seemed as if he sneaked around in his own house."

She wrote about Chuck and physical violence: "He tried to choke me one time because I would not get on my knees and tell him he was superior to me because he was a man. He ran after me to the bedroom and started to choke me. . . . He yelled at me *a lot* if I did not clean the house fast enough or if I ate too much. . . ."

She wrote about the threats: "His only other means of keeping me, and these worked, were telling me that a big honcho in the Mafia owed him a favor and he would have me killed."

She wrote about Chuck's idea of love: "He spoke often about loving me and after I crossed him one time he said the bubble had burst and I would have to work extra hard to convince him that I loved him. . . . One fight was because I would not tell him I loved him as much as he would like me to."

She talked about finally escaping, running away from him and leaving her clothes behind: "He said something about sending my clothes, but of course he didn't. I noticed when I was living with him there were all sorts of female clothes in boxes. I thought later that I was not the first lady to leave in a hurry."

The most recent news story I read about Chuck Traynor appeared in the New York Daily *News*. It may seem a non sequitur, a shaggy-dog ending. To me it seems strangely right. This is the story, quoted in its entirety.

"Marilyn Chambers, who was a porn movie queen, now is in business. She and husband Chuck Traynor are selling machine guns which they manufacture along with a silent partner."

thirty-eight

I've always felt you get what's coming to you. If you do well, you'll be rewarded. If you do evil, that's what you'll get in return. So what has happened to the other figures from my past? The men who destroyed years of my life and then haunted my nightmares.

For some the punishment has already begun. Consider the men who profited most from *Deep Throat*. And profited is the right word. The producers of *Deep Throat* have made as much money as some countries spend on their national budget.

These men are members of the Peraino family. I got to know Lou ("Butchie") Peraino, a 250-pound hulk who borrowed $25,000 from his father, an investment that has

returned a profit that some estimate to be in the neighborhood of $300,000,000. It has been widely reported that the
Perainos were mob-connected.

Chuck Traynor denies that fact. Here is how he
described the porno business to the Los Angeles *Free Press*:
"It is a business operation. I've been in and out of the
porno business since 1960. It's operated mostly by younger
guys who've seen maybe 500 nude girls and are not
overwhelmed by a naked body. And there's no casting
couch because there's not time for that sort of thing. People
say 'It's the Mafia.' That's bullshit. I was production
manager on *Deep Throat*, and people said that was a syndi-
cate film. It's not."

Let me tell you what bothers me most about this particular lie: It covers up one of the most powerful arguments
against pornography. Because the truth is that the Perainos
are mob-connected; the truth is that the money made by
Deep Throat, and indirectly by me, has poured into Mafia
coffers; the truth is, furthermore, if you are involved in the
pornography business, the odds are very good you are
involved with mobsters. And this is the bottom line: If you
buy a ticket to a pornographic movie, some of that money
probably goes directly to the Mafia.

Pornography today is reported to be at least a $7 billion
a year business—and it is estimated that half of that money
goes to the Mafia. According to government officials, only
gambling and narcotics supply more money to the crime
industry than pornography. The connection between pornography and organized crime becomes stronger every
year.

The *Deep Throat* story began with that modest investment by "Big Tony" Peraino, a man now in his seventies.
Printed reports reveal that both "Big Tony" and his
brother, Joe are "made" members of the Joseph Colombo
"family"—one of New York's five Mafia families. And the
three Perainos—Lou, his father Anthony, his uncle
Joseph—were the ones who most profited from *Deep
Throat*.

However, *Deep Throat* has been to them what gold was to Midas, both their fortune and their undoing.

Lou ("Butchie") Peraino got into the pornography business early. He was first arrested at the age of 26 when he owned something called All-State Film Labs, a company that divided its time between the processing of straight and porno movies. The charge: possession of obscene movies, a charge that was later thrown out on a technicality.

In 1971 Lou's career was to take a sudden upward turn. This was because three careers were to suddenly come together and blossom, if that word can be used in this context. Lou Peraino had just started a porno company—Gerard Damiano Film Productions, Inc.—with Gerry Damiano, a former Brooklyn hairdresser.

Their very first feature, an 8-millimeter cheapie-quickie entitled *Sex U.S.A.* starred Harry Reems and a certain Linda Lovelace. As the new film executives saw my little deep-throat freak show for the first time, it gave them their basic concept for *Deep Throat.*

In the beginning the Peraino's owned two-thirds of the movie and Damiano owned one-third. In 1972 Damiano sold his full interest in the movie (eventually worth somewhere between $50 million and $100 million) to Lou Peraino for a grand total of $25,000. Damiano never explained why he settled for such a pittance. And, when a reporter pressed him on the matter, he said: "You want me to get both my legs broken?"

How much money did the Perainos make on *Deep Throat*?

No one knows for sure. The best answers have been provided by a team of investigative reporters, Bill Knoedelseder and Ellen Farley, who have reported on the Perainos in a detailed series of articles, *Family Business*, that ran in the Los Angeles *Times*. The money that *Deep Throat* earned was largely cash. The reporters described how some of that cash was handled.

They quoted movie distributor Fred Biersdorf describing the scene in Lou Peraino's office as the money began rolling in: "I was like a kid in Disneyland. Everything was strictly cash. I mean, if someone wanted a mink coat, they'd just walk into Bonwit Teller and plop down $18,000 or $20,000 in cash."

Biersdorf once asked Joseph Peraino how much money the film had brought in. The answer: "Well, Lou's got eight kids and Joe [Lou's brother] has kids, and their kids and their grandkids have nothing to worry about the rest of their lives. Does that tell you how much the movie brought in?"

Well, maybe not precisely—but it gives us some idea. And, in fact, it is known that the movie continues to make huge sums of money for the Mafia. A single theater in Hollywood, the Pussycat Theater, played the movie 13 times a day for ten years and reported a take of 6.4 million dollars. That's *one* theater. The videocassette, the best-selling sex videocassette of all time, has sold at least a half-million copies at $60 each.

One of the first things Lou Peraino did with his profits was to form an independent movie company, Bryanston Distributors Inc. This was followed, quickly, by investment companies, a yacht, porno movie theaters, record and music publishing companies.

From 1973 to 1976, during a time of economic doldrums in Hollywood, the new company was a quick success. Lou had always wanted to appear straight and (on the strength of the *Deep Throat* bankroll) he produced a series of exploitation films, everything from kung-fu epics (*Return of the Dragon*) to milestones of violence (*The Texas Chain Saw Massacre.*) The first-year profits were put at $20 million. Or as a headline in the trade paper *Variety* saw it: "Bryanston Boffo!"

While Bryanston was considered an up-and-coming concern, the California Department of Justice saw it differently; it placed the firm at the top of a list of mob-controlled corporations: "It appears that Bryanston coordinates the nationwide distribution of full-length films for organized crime."

As reporters Farley and Knoedelseder pointed out, the film that brought all the profits also began to bring trouble to the Perainos. In August of 1974 a federal grand jury in Memphis indicted all three Perainos on the charge of "transporting obscene materials"—*Deep Throat*, that is to say—across state lines.

This was another trial where the jury viewed the movie. And found it to be "obscene." At the end of April in 1976, the Perainos were all found guilty. "Big Tony" was on a yacht in the Bahamas but Lou and his uncle Joe were each sentenced to one year in prison, along with a series of fines. Joe's conviction was later overturned but Lou did spend time in prison. This ended the short reign of Bryanston pictures, although *Deep Throat* continued to do big business around the country.

The Perainos' troubles didn't end with that Memphis conviction. On Valentine's Day of 1980, precisely at noon, 400 FBI agents and police conducted a mammoth raid on porno movie theaters, warehouses, retail businesses and offices in 13 cities across the country. This was Operation Miporn (short for "Miami pornography"). Among the 40 individuals arrested in this round-up were two of the Perainos—Lou and his brother, Joe—and the charge was again interstate shipment of obscenity.

The following February Lou Peraino was sentenced in Miami to six years in prison (brother Joe received a three-year sentence). That same month, their father Anthony ("Big Tony") finally had to face the music in Memphis. He served 9½ months in prison and was charged a $15,000 fine.

* * *

When Chuck Traynor launched my pornography career he made me pose for obscene photographs taken by one Leonard Campagno, a.k.a. Lenny Camp. Investigative reporter Martin Yant reports that Lenny Camp has been arrested several times on pornography charges.

In one case, vice officers raided a Hollywood (Florida) apartment and arrested Campagno just as he was about to film a 15-year-old girl in a porno movie. On that occasion the officers removed truckloads of pornography from the apartment. In another case Campagno was charged with inducing a 16-year-old girl and a man to take part in a naked sex scene.

Typical. But you do get caught eventually. In 1975, he was found guilty of producing an obscene film and sentenced to 18 months in jail, the longest sentence ever given for a pornography conviction in Dade County.

* * *

Yant also tracked down Dr. B.G. Gross, the Miami doctor who injected my breasts with silicone. Gross was suspended for six months in 1977 for performing the same operations on at least 100 patients. Gross admitted doing the illegal operation on me but was angry that I had told about him: "Obviously, her career was finished and she was broke so she got a ghost writer to write a book trying to drum up her new career. She just wants the money she didn't make the first time around at others' expense."

* * *

Al Goldstein goes on publishing *Screw* and occasionally he'll talk about me. Each time he does, he reveals more about himself than he does about me. Here is a quote from a tape-recorded *Playboy* interview describing our first meeting.

"We met in a small, cold $17-a-night hotel room, and it was the most difficult interview I ever conducted, because she's really inarticulate. Chuck Traynor, then her husband and 'manager,' did most of the talking. After the interview, I said, 'Listen, I'd like you to suck my cock.' I figured she was just a hooker anyway, so I wasn't embarrassed. She said fine, Chuck said OK, and she blew me. . . . I ran the photos of her sucking my cock and my description of it. It was a paradigm of personal journalism."

So much for Al Goldstein's concept of journalism, personal or otherwise.

* * *

Hugh Hefner, publisher of *Playboy*, has also had his bad moments. Hollywood director Peter Bogdanovich's book about the murder of former Playmate-of-the-Year Dorothy Stratton (*The Killing of the Unicorn*) examined Hefner's role in Stratton's life.

Shortly thereafter Hefner suffered a mild stroke, a stroke he blamed on the stress created by Bogdanovich's book. He seems to have recovered and recent statements indicate that the *Playboy* publisher has undertaken a serious reappraisal of his life; I hope this is true. He recently began work on his own life story, so we'll know more then.

* * *

And, finally, Linda Lovelace—where is *she* today?

Nowhere. Linda Lovelace seems finally to have been put out of her misery. And Linda Marchiano has a much keener understanding of who she is, where she is and where she is going.

No longer do I suffer through my old nightmare, the one where five faceless strangers appear around my bed. My nightmares now are standard nightmares, *normal* nightmares, nightmares *anyone* might have.

What causes fear? I think it's the unknown. For much of my life I didn't know who I was. And maybe that was the reason for much of the fear.

What has caused me to define myself? Life itself defines you, tells you who and what you are. Being the wife of a decent and hard-working man helps define me. Being the mother to two loving and good children helps define me, too. Fitting into a community, being a good neighbor, being involved with my children's education—this is all part of the picture of my life now, all part of my new family album.

thirty-nine

Sometimes I even forget to be afraid. The other day, I heard a noise out in the backyard. As I came out to the yard, a man—a stranger—was just rounding the corner of our house. I snapped at him: "Who are you and what do you want?" and only then did I stop to wonder why my Doberman guard dog was being unnaturally quiet. However, he quickly produced his credentials; he was from the Internal Revenue Service and apologized for the intrusion. This, too, is a sign of normality. Nothing strikes more fear in our hearts these days than a visit from the IRS.

Old fears are not completely gone and probably never will be. Not as long as certain people are free to walk the streets. However, no longer does the fear paralyze me. It causes me to speak up, to fight back, to protect myself.

As I've come to know myself, others have, too. Writing *Ordeal* was like coming out of the closet, finally exposing myself. My neighbors would now know that I had been Linda Lovelace—*the* Linda Lovelace—and how would they react to that?

Would they ask us to leave the community? Would the old cycle start again? The Marchianos had finally found a place they could fit in; would Linda Lovelace ruin that? This time it didn't work out that way. I know everyone on the block and they've all offered us a warm handshake and a nice hello. Our next-door neighbors, Born Again Christians, kept their distance for many months when we first moved here. They didn't know whether we'd be okay or not. It took a while but I guess we passed their tests, because now we're friends.

Knowing that I have the support of my neighbors helps keep the fear at arm's length. Larry, too, feels much safer.

If there were any incidents with the neighbors, that would be different. But the whole town seems to like me and I return the feeling.

And part of my security comes from my children. I'm so proud of them. Dominic is a regular take-charge guy, very responsible. And my daughter Lindsay just amazes me. She could be struggling to climb a tree and if you go to help her, she pushes you away. She's as independent as a person can be. Which reminds me: I've got to write Gloria a letter because I give her a lot of credit for that. The big danger in raising a child is that you'll make them overly dependent on someone else, even their parents.

What do I want for my kids more than anything else? Common sense. Intelligence. Decency. (Oh, I guess I wouldn't mind it very much if my daughter married an Arabian oil magnate so that she could take care of her mother and her father in their old age—sorry about that, Gloria.)

When you stop to think about it, I was raised in a way that almost guaranteed I'd never be independent. Now a major part of my life—it's a strong enough feeling to be almost religious with me—has to do with independence. Oh, I'm still a traditionalist. No one celebrates a holiday—a birthday, Christmas, Easter—with more enthusiasm than I do.

Religion? I concluded my last book on a religious note and that led many people to ask whether I was a Born Again Christian. Well, I'm a free human being now so I was born again and I do believe in God. To me, that's enough. He and I have been talking for a long time, a long time by ourselves, and I wouldn't want to do any preaching to anyone else. After all, I don't much care for it when someone preaches at me. If you've got something that works for you, that's fine—keep it. I've got something that works for me; I'll keep that.

And much of my strength comes from Larry. We've aged a bit but then, we've gone through quite a bit. Still, the love is there. My attitude toward man-woman relationships remains traditional. Once my whole dream was to get married, have a home and have children—period. That's still important to me and I'm happy with the way things are right now.

However, happy homemaker is just part of the picture. While a typical day might include driving the children to school; it might also include a visit to a nearby college to deliver a lecture. My husband goes off to work and does his nine-to-five thing—whether it's putting in insulation, spackling walls or installing television cable—and I take care of the two children.

However, there have been some changes. In the first place, I refuse to be totally dependent on anyone else. The way I avoid it is to make sure my role at home doesn't become unimportant or trivial.

That's why I handle the money. Larry comes home after a tough week's work and he hands me his pay. I deposit the money, write the checks, pay the bills and watch where every penny goes. It's possible that until now I wasn't ready for this. Before meeting Larry, I didn't want to *know* about handling money.

One snapshot you *won't* see in the Marchiano family album is the picture of my husband Larry, wearing an apron, in the kitchen doing the cooking. I know mine isn't a very "liberated" attitude, and maybe all husbands *should* help with the cooking—but whenever he goes near the kitchen he makes a mess. Really.

And right over there you'll see a picture of me *not* vacuuming the house every day. I'm still pretty much of a homebody, a person who likes the home to be neat and clean. but I've learned that there's a pricetag on that kind of thing and sometimes it's more than I care to pay. Reviewers had fun with the part of my last book where I said that I could be happy just vacuuming my home. Well, that was the truth. Then.

My whole attitude toward man-woman relationships has

changed. I think of my neighbor and friend, Francine, who has five small children. Her husband Fred works very long hours, lives a limited life and expects her to do the same. I tried to get her to join a school group with me, and Fred wouldn't let her go. I was shocked. I even did something I don't usually do; I butted in. I asked Francine this: What right does he have *not* to let her go? What right does any man have?

"Oh, you know Fred," she told me, "he's just a typical old-fashioned husband—he has a wife and a nice family and a home and he goes out and works for them and the wife stays in the home."

"In time that'll change," I predicted.

"I wonder," she said.

And so do I. The way things now are, she'll never find out who she is. Not really. She's being kept like a child, like a prisoner. And I can see this possibly going on the rest of her life. There's only one way she exists; she exists in relationship to another person. And to me that's the same as being in bondage.

I don't call myself a feminist because I don't like labels. However, I did and do support the Equal Rights Amendment. All that says is that people should be equal under the law. I've always felt men and women should be treated the same. Maybe it seems silly to need a law to spell that out but, believe me, it *does* have to be spelled out in the law. Otherwise, some men will never admit that women are their equals.

Larry's not like that. Since our darkest days together, he has mellowed out considerably. Deep down, Larry will always have enormous resentment. Almost all of it is directed against the men who kept me prisoner and profited from my imprisonment. But some, I suspect, is directed at me; very few men could adjust to sharing life with a woman who has gone through as much as I have.

Larry is a macho man; he has strong opinions and he's quick to act on them. But living with me, living through

these experiences, has been an education for both of us. He
may be macho but he calls himself a feminist—and he is.

And as long as I've been bringing up snapshots from the
family album, here's the one I've been saving for last. This
is a recent picture, one that makes me extraordinarily
proud. One that makes me feel truly . . . out of bondage.

You would see me in this one surrounded by United
States Senators. Just this past September I was called to
testify before The Senate Subcommittee on Juvenile Justice
when it was holding hearings on pornography. The official
title: *Effect of Pornography on Women and Children*.

I know I wasn't the committee's most intellectual or
well-informed witness—but apparently I was able to fill in
some gaps for them. I could tell them what it was like to be
caught in the pornographic web. I didn't speak as an educated person but as a victim and survivor.

As I testified—as I realized where I was speaking—I
became very emotional. Never before had I been this close
to the power to do good, the power to expose pornography.
And although I was testifying about my most awful experiences, although I was describing a life of total degradation,
I never felt better.

"We have gone from the acceptability of *Deep Throat* in
1972, to child pornography, to snuff movies, and the muti-
lation of women in 1983 in Arizona, to the sexual abuse of
young children in our day care centers, by city employees
in the city of New York. My question is: What is next?"

Then it was time to answer to committee's questions.

"So your basic point is that *Deep Throat* got $600 million
and you got a lot of bruises?" Senator Specter asked.

"That is *not* the main point," I said. "The main point is
that they took a human being and through pain and degredation and beatings and constant threats, forced me to do
something that I never would have become involved in,
had it not been for a .45 put to my head."

"And what is your response," the senator asked, "to
those who say that the movies like *Deep Throat* ought to be

permitted to be shown, under the Constitutional protection of the First Amendment?"

"And what about *my* First Amendment rights?" The Senate of the United States may not be the best place to express anger or emotion but I was both angry and emotional. "What about my rights as a human being? You know, it is not fair. Like I said before, everytime someone watches that film, they are watching me being raped, and I am trying to teach my children good, and then they turn around and see that I was raped, I was beaten, and that film is still allowed to be shown, and people are still making money off of it, and my family and my children and I are suffering because of it. It is not fair. It's is inhumane."

Giving testimony—perhaps that is what my life is all about now. This book is part of that testimony. I've been invited to speak to another Congressional committee—and I'll be proud to be there. Over the next few years I intend to take my testimony to college campuses and towns across the country; anywhere people are concerned about pornography and what it is doing to us.

And I expect my message will be the same simple one that it is now.

Don't believe it when they tell you pornography is a "victimless crime."

I was one of its victims.

I'm not any more.